DISPOSED OF
BY LIBRARY
HOUSE OF LORDS

D0553370

Inside the BBC

INSIDE THE
B B C
British Broadcasting
Characters

Leonard Miall

FOREWORD BY
Kenneth Harris

Weidenfeld and Nicolson, London

All of the photographs are used by kind
permission of the BBC Photograph Library

Copyright © 1994 by Leonard Miall
First published in Great Britain in 1994
by Weidenfeld & Nicolson Ltd
Orion House
5 Upper Saint Martin's Lane
London WC2H 9EA

All rights reserved. No part of this publication
may be reproduced, stored in a retrieval system, or
transmitted in any form or by any means, electronic,
mechanical, photocopying, recording or otherwise,
without the prior permission of the copyright owner

Leonard Miall has asserted his moral right to be
identified as the author of this work

A catalogue reference is available from
the British Library

ISBN 0 297 81328 5

Filmset by Selwood Systems, Midsomer Norton
Printed in Great Britain by Butler & Tanner Ltd,
Frome and London

To Sally

Contents

Foreword
Kenneth Harris

Leonard Miall has lived three different lives in the BBC, and has acquired knowledge and wisdom in all of them. He has been a pioneer foreign correspondent; an executive running Television Talks and Current Affairs, rapidly transforming that department into the Corporation's flagship; and, as an elder statesman, he has been the Research Historian, preparing the material for several of the books of BBC history written by Lord Briggs. This personal account of developments inside the BBC, expressed through portraits of some of his colleagues who made the Corporation what it has been at its best, combines the techniques of autobiography, memoir and history, without the limitations from which these vehicles sometimes suffer. In it Miall also modestly gives something of himself.

When in 1950 I first met Leonard Miall in person – I say 'in person' because like millions of others I had been listening to his authoritative baritone broadcasts from America for many years – he was the BBC's news correspondent in Washington. Some would say that his time there, from 1945 to 1953, was his finest hour. They were years fraught with the problems of America's evolving post-war relationship with Europe. From the United

Kingdom's point of view, they were perhaps the most important years of the century.

Some would say – I certainly would – that Miall was the best correspondent the BBC has ever had in Washington. That is perhaps debatable, but nobody can deny that at that demanding time in the history of Anglo-American relations no British journalist in Washington was as well informed about what was going on behind the scenes of the most powerful capital in the world as he was. This was partly due to the incomparable reputation of the BBC at that time, but also due in part to Miall's personal reputation. After all it is on the reputations of the Leonard Mialls of this world that the BBC's public reputation has been founded.

The outstanding example of what he was able to achieve for the BBC is the role he played in the Marshall Plan which might be said to have influenced the course of history. An offer was made by General George Marshall, then the American Secretary of State, when he was given an honorary degree at Harvard University on 5 June 1947. His speech was virtually ignored by the American press, and by most British correspondents. The British Embassy in Washington sent its text to the Foreign Office by slow diplomatic bag rather than by telegraph, in order to save scarce dollars. However, Miall happened to be broadcasting the weekly talk *American Commentary* that evening and he emphasised the urgent importance of what Marshall had just said.

It had been known for some weeks that the Democratic American administration was considering economic assistance to the war-torn countries of Europe to enable them to recover, provided they could come forward with a co-operative continental plan which an economy-minded Republican Congress would approve. Miall was able in his talk to stress two points not directly mentioned by General Marshall. He had been privately briefed shortly beforehand by Marshall's deputy, Dean Acheson, who later became Miall's personal friend.

The interpretations included in Miall's broadcast were, first, that the offer – not yet known as the Marshall Plan – to provide massive European help was now official American policy, and, second, that the Truman administration would only be able to secure Congressional support for that policy if the countries of Europe responded promptly that they would come forward with a concerted plan. He made both these points loud and clear. Ernest Bevin, the Foreign Secretary, happened to be listening to Miall's *American Commentary* in bed that evening. As he later said, Marshall's offer came like a lifebelt thrown to a drowning man. He grabbed it 'with both hands'. Despite the absence of a message from the Embassy, Bevin took action first thing the next morning, setting up a meeting with the French Foreign Secretary. The Marshall Plan was born.

When I arrived in Washington I saw a good deal of Miall – he was very kind and helpful to beginners – but I did not learn about his 1947 broadcast on the Marshall Plan until twenty years later. I heard it then from the horse's mouth. In January 1971 I was in Washington to record an interview with Dean Acheson for the BBC. After it was over we had dinner and reminisced about his days at the State Department. Miall's name came up very often. On the subject of the Marshall Plan broadcast Dean Acheson said: 'It was a good thing that Leonard did not lose his voice that night, or his nerve.'

Leonard Miall was not the doyen of the British Washington correspondents, since two of them had been there longer, but – in spite of some jealousy – he was the most liked and respected of them. He was on very good terms with the many correspondents of newspapers from all over the United States who headed bureaux in Washington. They sometimes found the attitude of British newspapermen to Americans living out in the sticks rather patronising. But Miall combined two things that they liked: he was very British, yet he was very pro-American, having spent a considerable time in various posts of the United States before being sent as the BBC's first peacetime correspondent. This gave him a perspective on American affairs which is still unrivalled, except in another sphere of American reportage by the fabulous Alistair Cooke. Always perceptive, and sometimes critical, Miall was also urbane, good-humoured and benign – characteristics which did not prevent him from occasionally clashing with his bosses in London, including the Editor of BBC News, an episode described in this book.

When Miall returned to Britain he took the lead in establishing many of the main television current affairs, arts and science programmes which have made the BBC famous throughout the world today. His most important contribution was to the development of political television. Before he took over, that field was restricted by all manner of regulations, conventions and practices which existed to suit the government and opposition of the day. Drawing extensively on his experiences of political television in the United States, Miall made the British programmes altogether less of a public relations exercise and much more like the genuine television journalism which we know today.

Previously Talks and Current Affairs interviewers tended to behave with great deference to politicians and virtually confined themselves to asking questions which

their 'guests' would condescend to answer. Long before
Miall left the department to organise the launch of BBC2,
they were asking the questions which viewers wanted
answered, and not pulling their forelocks in the course of
doing it. His seminal work was done before Independent
Television had come into existence. He played a great
part in creating the climate in which interviewers such
as Robin Day, John Freeman and Ludovic Kennedy or
producers in his department like Huw Wheldon and Paul
Fox could flourish. His account of the ups and downs is
revealing, enlightening and predictably amusing. Equally
predictably, it is too self-effacing for my liking.

By writing about these matters he has made a most
valuable contribution to the history of British television;
and since British television has, for better or for worse,
greatly influenced the course of British politics – it has
made some political leaders and unmade others – he has
also contributed to the history of the country. There is
more to be learned, understood, praised, and criticised,
about the BBC in this book than in any other I have read.

Introduction

The Granta, the Cambridge undergraduate journal, published a profile of me the term that I was President of the Union and editor of the *Cambridge Review*. It described me as a 'supreme jack of all trades' and predicted that I would finish up in the BBC.

Two years later, just after the Munich crisis in 1938, the BBC advertised a vacancy for a Press Officer at a salary of £6 a week. I was one of 3,000 people who applied. There was much unemployment at the time, and the BBC was considered a glamorous place to work. Moreover, £6 would be a welcome 20 per cent increase on what I was then being paid. I listed my qualifications, including the fact that I knew German, which was not relevant for the job of Press Officer, but I put it in for good measure. After a few weeks I was shortlisted for an interview by an appointments board.

I learned afterwards that I was one of the last two, but eventually I received the self-addressed envelope thanking me for applying and saying the vacancy had been filled. I was terribly depressed. I had set my heart on getting into the BBC. A few weeks later, early in 1939, I received another letter from the Appointments Officer. It said there was a vacancy for someone to run its news talks in German and if I would like to be considered for it would I please telephone immediately, and hold myself free for an interview with an appointments board the next day. The salary would be 10 guineas a week – more than twice what I was then earning.

Of course I telephoned Broadcasting House straight away, and within twenty-four hours I was appointed – no weeks of delay this time. With war clouds looming, the Foreign Office had urgently requested the BBC to supplement its news in German, which had been started just before the Munich Agreement, with a daily programme of news talks. That is how I came to join the BBC in such a hurry.

As *Granta* said, I have been a jack of all trades. I was a founder member of the European Service which played such an important role during the Second World War. From external broadcasting I moved into domestic radio as one of the BBC's first foreign correspondents, and was in Washington in the exciting years immediately after the war. I transferred from radio into television just as the balance of their relative importance tilted. I was actively involved, both at home and abroad, with the BBC's international role in the broadcasting world.

These sketches of some of the people who made the BBC great are arranged to provide an outline history of its first half-century. I have had the luck to know every Director-General since the BBC was founded, and have worked closely with many of them. Several are portrayed here, along with other colleagues who made important contributions to the BBC's unique position in the broadcasting world. The selection is arbitrary. There are very many others, particularly women, who have played important roles in establishing the BBC's status. They are omitted only because I did not work with them as closely as I did with those who appear in these pages. There are also many areas of broadcasting, particularly in music, drama, education and, above all, engineering, that are inadequately represented. This in no way means that I underrate their importance.

There are many reasons why I enjoyed my varied life in the BBC. For a newsman, it was gratifying to work in an organisation whose news integrity was respected throughout the world. As a foreign correspondent I was never given a special line to follow when reporting a story, unlike many of my newspaper colleagues.

By the same token, current affairs programmes, with which I was closely involved, had to be scrupulously fair – something not always easy to achieve. And programmes about science or medicine or archaeology had to have the same integrity. Fortunately we were able to call on many experts who helped with disinterested advice. Of course we made mistakes from time to time. Sometimes external ground rules caused difficulties. Lawyers and doctors in private practice were originally not allowed by their professional authorities to appear on television because of their rules against advertising. Some people are clever at getting round such rules. During the war I encountered a San Francisco dentist who had changed his name by deed poll to Painless Parker. Was that advertising? Then there was the iniquitous 'Fourteen-Day Rule' by which the political parties sought to bolster the supremacy of Parliament by preventing current affairs programmes from discussing topical issues before they were debated in the House of Commons.

BBC Television prided itself on becoming the greatest stage for drama. When I was Assistant Controller of Programme Services at Television Centre I learned to appreciate the highly professional management skills involved in these major dramatic productions. A script had to be commissioned, perhaps two years ahead. Actors had to be cast and contracted. Scenery, costumes and properties had to be designed, made or hired, location scenes selected with appropriate reference to the time of year. If the action is supposed to be at Christmas time, there must not be leaves on the trees. Casts and technical crews must be available. Rehearsals had to be held, often in halls inconveniently far away and later in the studios themselves. Scenery had to be set and lighting adjusted. Appropriate publicity material and billings for the *Radio Times* had to be prepared. Before pre-recording was developed, these and other activities, all operating to different time scales, had to be co-ordinated so that each individual ingredient of these elaborate productions was ready to go when the televised clock reached the precise second for transmission. Television Centre is a programme factory, but few industrial factories have to meet such a tight delivery schedule.

Entertainment programmes have been the backbone of the BBC from its very outset. Zany radio comedies blossomed during the war. ITMA and Much-Binding-in-the-Marsh did as much for morale during the blitz as Vera Lynn's songs and J. B. Priestley's *Postscripts*. Later came *The Goon Show* and *Monty Python's Flying Circus*. Hancock transferred from radio to television and was joined by *Steptoe and Son*, *Morecambe and Wise*, *The Two Ronnies*, *Dad's Army*, *'Allo 'Allo* and a host of others which kept the country laughing, and devastated cinema attendance.

But splendid as the programmes are as home entertainment, the real magic of television is watching the live event, whether it be sport or ceremonial, a major debate in the House of Commons or a man stepping for the first time on to the surface of the moon. Never before have the broad masses of the people, virtually all round the world, been able to watch history being made. The BBC has always been willing to alter its programme schedule to allow the live coverage of any significant event.

On the BBC's fortieth anniversary, when I was helping to organise the planning of BBC2, I gave the first of the BBC Lunchtime Lectures. Its title was 'The Future of BBC Television'. I ended it with these words:

The television of the future must not sink to becoming merely the vehicle of a sales campaign, or a political method of fooling some of the people most of the time. It must not pander to lust and sadism, or perhaps worst of all, to triviality. The television of the future must serve the needs of the viewers of the future; needs for relaxation and for laughter, for answers to some of man's eternal quest for greater knowledge of the world he lives in; needs for pity and gladness and for gaiety, and for that enrichment of the spirit which comes from contact with a mind of quality or a thing of great beauty. These are the ends that the television of the future must serve; and it will be by these standards that our achievements are measured by our successors forty years on.

November 1993

Leonard Miall
BBC Career

1939–42 EUROPEAN SERVICE

1939   Inaugurated news talks broadcast to Europe
1941   German Talks and Features Editor

1942–45 seconded to POLITICAL WARFARE EXECUTIVE (PWE)

1942   New York office, British Political Warfare Mission to the United States (BPWM)
1943   Director of News, San Francisco office, BPWM
1944   Head of New York office, BPWM
            Personal Assistant to Deputy Director-General, PWE London
1945   Psychological Warfare Division of Supreme Headquarters, Allied Expeditionary Force, Luxembourg

1945–53 NEWS DIVISION

1945   Special correspondent, Czechoslovakia

Acting diplomatic correspondent
1945–53   Washington correspondent

1954–66 TELEVISION SERVICE

1954–61   Head of Television Talks and Documentaries
1961   Assistant Controller, Current Affairs and Talks
          Awarded OBE
1962–63   Special Assistant to Director of Television,
          planning the start of BBC2
          Inaugurated BBC Lunchtime Lectures
1963–66   Assistant Controller, Programme Services
(1965   Adviser, Committee on Broadcasting, New
          Delhi)
(1966   Editor, *Richard Dimbleby, Broadcaster*)

1966–74 OVERSEAS AND FOREIGN RELATIONS DIVISION

1966–71   Representative in the United States
(1970   Awarded Certificate of Appreciation, New
          York City)
1971–74   Controller, Overseas and Foreign Relations
1974   Retired from the full-time staff

1975–84 PUBLIC AFFAIRS DIVISION

1975–84   Research Historian
          Worked with Asa Briggs on preparing *The
          History of Broadcasting in the United Kingdom,
          Volume IV*, 1979; *Governing the BBC* 1979; *The
          BBC: The First Fifty Years*, 1985.

Inside the BBC

1

John Reith

'Life was meant for living.'

John Charles Walsham Reith, 1st Baron, PC, GCVO, GBE, KT, CB, Kt, DCL, born 20 July 1889, married 1921 Muriel Odhams, one son one daughter; General Manager, BBC 1922, Managing Director 1923, Director-General 1927–38; chairman: Imperial Airways 1938–39, BOAC 1939–40; Minister of Information 1940, Minister of Transport 1940, Minister of Works and Buildings 1940–42; Captain RNVR 1943–45; chairman, Commonwealth Telecommunications Board 1946–50; Lord Rector, Glasgow University 1965–68; Lord High Commissioner of the General Assembly of the Church of Scotland 1967–68; numerous honorary degrees; died 16 June 1971, aged 81.

One day in the early 1960s I received an unexpected message from the office of the BBC's Director-General, then Hugh Carleton Greene. Would I and my wife please cancel any engagements we might have for the following Thursday and go instead to Royal Ascot? The BBC would pay for any formal clothes we might need to hire.

Peter Dimmock's new contract for the coverage of the races at Ascot had included a private box, which was normally used by the Governors and the Director-General

1

for high-level entertaining. But that particular Thursday – Gold Cup Day – there was an important Board Meeting at which the Governors were due to review the BBC's long-term budget. All the top brass were standing by to protect their particular corners, so the box had been offered to the Assistant Head of Television Outside Broadcasts, Harry Middleton, whose special responsibility was horse racing. Middleton had arranged to entertain two important racing contacts from Newbury and Cheltenham and their wives to lunch.

However, Lord Reith, the first Director-General, had just telephoned to ask whether he might bring a friend to watch the races from the BBC's box, Reith had been invited to join the lunch, and it was felt that Middleton might welcome some help in looking after the BBC's founding father. I was Head of Television Talks, the term then used for the factual programme, and was not involved in the vital budget review. Hence my summons to a day at the races.

I had joined the BBC less than a year after Reith left it. His aura still dominated Broadcasting House, but I had never met him. My mental picture was of a strong leader, albeit a rather dour son of the manse, who never allowed drinks to be served on BBC premises, or starting prices to be broadcast, and whose staff knew that to be cited in a divorce action could mean immediate dismissal.

Reith arrived at the box just after we got there, a very impressive figure. He stood 6 feet 6 inches tall, his strong craggy face scarred on the left side where a First World War bullet had seriously wounded him. He was immaculately dressed for the occasion in a grey morning suit, and was accompanied by an attractive dark-haired girl who was introduced to us as his goddaughter, Dawn Mackay. We enjoyed a delicious cold lunch, at which Reith partook of several glasses of champagne. We applauded as the Queen drove down the course in her open carriage, and then the racing began.

Fortunately the pundits from Newbury and Cheltenham seemed to know precisely which horse was going to win each race, and they kindly marked the cards for Reith and me. We went off together to the tote and placed our bets. Seldom throughout the afternoon were we disappointed. Between races we sipped whiskies and sodas and enjoyed chatting with the charming girl Reith had brought with him. After the last race I drove home, considerably better off than when I arrived, having spent a delightful afternoon at my first visit to Ascot, but with all my preconceptions of Lord Reith totally shattered.

Reith admitted to John Freeman in a *Face to Face* interview that he was fairly old before he appreciated that 'life was meant for living', which, no doubt, included enjoying champagne and a flirtatious afternoon at the races with a girl who infatuated him for several years at this stage of his life. When the *Face to Face* team called at his office to take a still photograph of him (he had asked for the cover of the *Radio Times* but had to settle for that of *The Listener*) there was a framed picture of Dawn Mackay on his desk. He asked whether it would be seen in *The Listener* photograph. On being told that it probably would, he put it away in a desk drawer – and then brought it out again, put it back on the desk and placed a bowl of heather in front of it.

Reith's behaviour vacillated between extremes. At his best, as on that afternoon at Ascot, he was charming, effervescent and excellent company. At his worst he was morose and consumed by self-pity, as can be seen from his extensive diaries, now in the BBC's Written Archives Centre, and painstakingly combed by Ian McIntyre for his recent biography *The Expense of Glory*. A similar picture emerges from the cringing letters Reith wrote during the war to Winston Churchill, whom he had previously despised, which are in the Public Record Office. It is sad that gloom and resentment dominated the second half of his life, depreciating the outstanding success of his previous attainments.

Here is a personal example. When I edited the memorial book *Richard Dimbleby, Broadcaster* in 1966, I quoted this recollection by a colleague who had been the chief sub-editor when Dimbleby began his career:

He very nearly didn't make it. His very first broadcast in the nine-thirty news was heard by the Director-General, then Sir John Reith, to us both a deeply respected and a rather frightening man. The newsroom phone rang three times, the signal that the DG was on the line. He enquired the name of the reporter in the News, and, on being told, said only that he never wanted to hear him again. But Dimbleby was given another chance and matters arranged themselves.

At the time the Dimbleby book appeared Reith had quarrelled with most of the people he still knew in the BBC, but he wrote to John Arkell, a member of the Board of Management with whom he remained on friendly terms. Three people, he said, had told him that he was reported to have said that he never wanted to hear Dimbleby again. Reith went on:

If this report be true, and if the statement be true, I suppose it was put in to discredit me. Do you approve of that? On the lowest terms, wouldn't you have thought I should have been informed and given opportunity to comment?

But is it true – the statement alleged to be given in the book? I have no recollection of it whatever. Might I be given the date of this broadcast – Mr D's first; and might I be given evidence that I made that remark? And if the date was after my departure, or if there is no evidence, I wonder what you think should be done.

I drafted a reply for Arkell to quote to his touchy complainant. After mentioning that I had again checked it with the writer, and had myself heard Dimbleby speak of it, I added:

Surely the point of this little story, read in context, is only that Dimbleby, at 23 with no experience of broadcasting at all, had with commendable enterprise created a job for himself which involved his reporting in his own voice alongside such men as Stuart Hibberd and John Snagge. That Dimbleby should not have been entirely successful at his very first attempt is not surprising. That the DG should have commented on a poor performance surely reflects no discredit on either of them. Of course, taken out of context, this minor incident has provided a talking point for some journalists.

John Charles Walsham Reith was the son of a Scottish Free Church Minister, and was trained as a civil engineer. He had had a good war record, but he was out of work in the autumn of 1922 when he noticed an advertisement for the post of General Manager of the newly formed British Broadcasting Company Ltd. He knew nothing about radio, but he was appointed, at the age of 33, and told: 'We're leaving it all to you. You'll be reporting at our monthly meetings and we'll see how you are getting on.' That kind of free hand was just what suited Reith.

The BBC Ltd was a private company formed by a consortium of the main radio manufacturers. Its purpose was to provide programmes so that the people buying the new wireless sets, with their headphones, their crystals and their cat's whiskers, should have something to tune into. The running costs came from the wireless licence collected

through the Post Office. Advertising revenue was pro-
hibited. The consortium of set manufacturers had put up
the capital. The purchase of a receiver included a so-called
'royalty payment', which also helped the new programming company to get going. An early complaint to
the BBC came from a listener who said he had paid for
his set 'including royalty'; he had by then had it several
months and not a single member of the Royal Family had
yet spoken on it.

The first broadcast was made on 14 November 1922.
Forty years later the BBC celebrated its anniversary by
instituting the Lunchtime Lectures in the Concert Hall of
Broadcasting House, and by holding a large reception at
Grocers' Hall in the City. It fell to me to give the inaugural
Lunchtime Lecture. Its title was 'The Future of BBC Tele-
vision', but before turning to my theme I cast a brief look
at the past of radio.

I recalled that well before the BBC became a public
corporation with a Royal Charter (a concept largely
devised by Reith himself) he had written a remarkable
book called *Broadcast over Britain*. In it Reith had declared:

Rightly or wrongly we took a comprehensive view of the possi-
bilities of broadcasting, and proceeded to explore and develop
these. Had we then been told that our ideas were extravagant,
and that we were to confine ourselves to the transmission of
concerts, then the service presumably would have been limited
to that, and although there is much merit in the transmission of
good concerts, the opportunity of the age would have passed.
No intimation, however, was received. The more we essayed to
do, the more encouragement in general was received.

I commented: 'Today, in this building, in this Concert
Hall, one can only salute with gratitude, the vision of
those who essayed to do so much and whose sights were
set so high.'

That evening Reith and I happened to leave the Grocers' Hall reception at the same time. He kindly offered me a lift in the enormous Rolls Royce provided for him by British Oxygen, the company of which he was vice-chairman at that time. I mentioned that I had been quoting from *Broadcast over Britain* in the Concert Hall that lunchtime, and the next day, when thanking him for going well out of his way to drop me at my door, I told him which passage I had quoted. Reith replied:

'I was most impressed and pleased, but to a degree also surprised, to hear you say that that afternoon you had been quoting from *Broadcast over Britain*. I wrote that book at the specific request of the Board; and I think the preface was headed Rothiemurchus, August 1924.

'What you quoted really makes good sense; but I would not have made such remarks a few years later; I would have said that, if there had been official notification of extravagance, I would have told them to mind their own business – the Corporation (as distinct from the Company) having far more responsibility and authority than a company did.'

The phrase 'I would have told them to mind their own business' is classic Reith.

When Reith ceased to be Director-General in June 1938 he was still only 48. He had had no precedents or standards to guide him. But he was determined from the outset to give broadcasting both status and purpose. During his sixteen years at the helm, the BBC had emerged from a small wireless operation at Marconi House serving Greater London into two radio networks covering the whole country. One was the National Programme, available to all and the same for everyone. The other was the Regional Programme, showing each region to itself, or exchanging programmes with the others.

However, Reith was determined that the development of regional broadcasting should not weaken the BBC as a unifying force for the nation.

Reith's BBC had also started the world's first regular high-definition television service in 1936, as well as a shortwave world service in English in 1932. It had created a great symphony orchestra and taken over the Proms. Moreover, it managed to educate many of us to love music. It published two successful magazines, the *Radio Times* and *The Listener*. Children's programmes, features, drama, schools programmes, running commentaries on ceremonies and sports events, dance music and variety all flourished, though Reith's strictly Calvinistic view of the right kind of programmes to hear on Sundays drove many listeners to sample the commercial alternative offered by Radio Luxembourg.

Reith himself had formulated the concept of public service broadcasting as the threefold requirement to inform, to educate and to entertain. BBC news was regarded as trustworthy. The government had originally decreed that talks, or lectures as they were first called, must not handle controversial subjects. Reith fought a long battle to get this restriction rescinded. Later he steered the BBC safely through the crises of the General Strike and the Abdication. He fought vigorously to preserve the BBC from political interference. The staff of four when he joined in 1922 had grown to 4,000 and the number of radio licences had risen from virtually nothing to nearly nine million. His concept of public service broadcasting had been widely copied in the Commonwealth.

He had personally formulated the BBC's ethos. In the summer of 1925 he gave evidence to the Crawford Committee, which was considering whether the private company should be converted into a public corporation.

He said, 'Unless you are convinced in your own soul that you are doing your duty to the world by working in the BBC for less than half the salary you would get elsewhere – don't stay.' His words have a somewhat hollow ring today.

Sir John Reith, as he became on 1 January 1927, the day that the private company's conversion into the British Broadcasting Corporation took effect, was in many ways an enlightened and imaginative employer. Janet Adam Smith, the talented assistant editor of *The Listener*, resigned early in April 1935, to marry a poet who was teaching at Newcastle upon Tyne. It was only a fortnight after the annual pay increases had been announced. She found that her salary had been given a substantial rise from £550 to £650. Her actual extra pay for her last two weeks' work only amounted to £4, but as she had already handed in her resignation she was surprised to receive an increase at all. When she went to say goodbye to Sir John he explained: 'In future you may want to do a job again, and they will say to you "What was your pay when you left the BBC?" and it would be better to say £650 than £550.' It was a kind action that had cost him little. He was always a canny Scot.

The pre-war BBC ran its own PAYE scheme long before the rest of the country, for Reith appreciated the difficulties his staff experienced in setting money aside for a large yearly tax payment. It was also one of the few organisations to operate a five-day working week, not five and a half days. And women were given equal pay with men for equal work. Reith established a generous pension fund to which staff and the Corporation both contributed, and he recognised early that programme staff needed an opportunity to recharge their creative batteries. He instituted a system known as grace leave which enabled staff to spend time abroad with the backing of a travel grant.

In other ways Reith was a less enlightened, indeed dictatorial, boss. He would not allow any kind of staff association or recognise trade union membership for BBC employees. The strict standards of his manse upbringing forced the resignation of his talented original chief engineer, Peter Eckersley, when he was about to be cited as the guilty party in a divorce action involving a fellow member of staff.

In 1936 pressure was put on Rex Lambert, the first editor of *The Listener*, to drop a civil action to clear his name. Lambert was threatening to sue Sir Cecil Levita, a former chairman of the London County Council, and was told by one of Reith's lieutenants that to pursue such an action might damage the BBC. Reith himself was not personally involved, but his paternalistic behaviour towards staff was to blame for the resulting uproar. It was particularly loud in the House of Commons, where Sir Stafford Cripps, during a debate on the renewal of the BBC's Charter, castigated Reith's methods of staff recruitment, the lack of machinery to air grievances, and the absence of established salaries and grades for different posts.

Despite the warning, Lambert went ahead with his action against Levita and collected huge damages, which Reith described as 'amazing and monstrous'. A subsequent inquiry into the various allegations against the BBC which had emerged in court led to many changes in its staff administration. It was about this time that Sir John began to look around for a new challenge. He was not fully stretched, he complained. He had partly organised himself out of a job, and he was bored. His expectations were not modest – Viceroy of India, ambassador to Washington, reorganiser of the War Office – he believed them all to be within his grasp.

In the end it took the Prime Minister, Neville Chamberlain, to persuade Reith that he should leave the BBC to become the chairman of Imperial Airways, the predecessor of British Airways. Did he fall, or was he pushed? In my view it was a bit of each. He was particularly annoyed at not being involved in the choice of his successor, and the decision to move out of the BBC soured the rest of his life. 'Stupendous folly', he called it.

Reith was later laden with honours of every kind, and he did useful work in both the public and the private sectors. But from then on his career was downhill. He complained that none of the various posts he held stretched him fully. He became a cantankerous curmudgeon, like one of his early bugbears on the first Board of Governors, Ethel Snowden, the wife of the Chancellor of the Exchequer in Ramsay MacDonald's Labour government, who was described by Lord Shinwell as 'fearsome when crossed, with an unerring knack of squeezing the last drop of drama out of the most trivial incident'. This trait in Reith's character sadly diminished the reputation he built by the creative work of his youth, although his creation remained and prospered.

2

Stuart Hibberd

*'The King's life is moving peacefully
towards its close.'*

*Andrew Stuart Hibberd, MBE 1935, born 5 September 1893,
married 1923 Alice Mary Chichester, no children; joined BBC
1924, retired as chief announcer 1951; publication: 'This – Is
London' 1950; died Budleigh Salterton, 1 November 1983,
aged 90.*

Stuart Hibberd was the golden voice of what Asa Briggs
has called the Golden Age of Wireless. He became the
chief announcer in 1924, though he was never officially
given that title, and he held the same post for twenty-six
years. The BBC announcers in those days were anonymous, but the press made his name well known, and he
enjoyed a remarkable place in the affection of his listeners,
both before and after the Second World War.

Hibberd's clear enunciation and his cultivated tenor
voice typified what was called the BBC accent. As the
Director-General said when Hibberd celebrated twenty-
five years at the BBC, his work 'brought happiness and
a sense of kindliness and companionship to millions of
people'.

Like many of Reith's early appointments, Hibberd had
been an officer during the First World War. He was a

West Countryman who had gone up to St John's College, Cambridge, with a Natural Sciences exhibition and had become one of four choral scholars. But after he had been only a year and a half at the university war broke out and Hibberd enlisted in the army. He was commissioned first into the Dorsets and then transferred to the Punjabi Regiment of the Indian Army, serving at Gallipoli and later in Mesopotamia and Waziristan. He became adjutant of his regiment and stayed in India until it was disbanded in 1922.

The D'Oyly Carte Opera Company at the Savoy Theatre in London auditioned Stuart Hibberd as a singer but he decided to take an offer of employment around the corner at Savoy Hill with the British Broadcasting Co. Ltd. He was then 31, a year younger than Reith had been on becoming the company's General Manager two years earlier. Hibberd's job was to present music programmes of all kinds, to introduce speakers, and to read the news.

Programmes from the studios at Savoy Hill ended around 10.30 p.m. Hibberd would then walk to the nearby Savoy Hotel to announce the dance band numbers, played by Debroy Somers or Carroll Gibbons, which ended the broadcasting day. He then had to hasten down the Strand to Charing Cross station to catch the last train back to his home in Kent. The railway staff, with whom he was very popular, would often delay the departure of the train until he showed up, racing along with his white silk evening scarf flying behind him.

It was not until 1926 that BBC announcers working in the evening began to wear dinner jackets, as a courtesy to the artists who came to broadcast or to the audiences at BBC concerts, many of whom were similarly clad. Hibberd, whose broadcasting diary formed the basis of his book *This – Is London*, wrote, 'Personally I have always thought it right and proper that announcers should wear evening dress when on duty.'

It is a widely believed myth that Reith made them wear evening dress to lend some kind of dignity or respectability to the news. In those days it was just a professional uniform, also worn by referees at prize fights. Actually Hibberd disliked wearing a dinner jacket when he read the news. He always used to gargle beforehand, and to loosen his collar and tie to prevent any constriction to his throat. Moreover, there was always the risk that the microphone might pick up the creak of a heavily starched shirt. The Prince of Wales had yet to make soft shirts acceptable with evening dress.

The news bulletins that Hibberd read were written in Reuters and dictated over the telephone to Savoy Hill. The newspaper proprietors, who controlled the news agencies, feared the potential competition of broadcasting. They would only supply the BBC with news from their agencies on condition that it was not broadcast before 6.30 p.m., by which time the evening papers were safely on the streets. It was 1927 before the first tape machine was installed on a permanent basis at Savoy Hill.

All these restrictive practices were perforce abandoned, though only temporarily, during the General Strike of 1926. In the small hours of 4 May Jack Payne's late-night dance music was interrupted for a special announcement carried by all transmitters. Reith himself broadcast the news that the strike had begun. It immediately closed down all the newspapers, except for a truncated version of *The Times*, the Communist *British Worker*, and the *British Gazette*, an emergency government propaganda sheet edited by the Chancellor of the Exchequer, Winston Churchill, from 11 Downing Street.

Broadcasting became overnight the most important national medium of communication. The news agencies agreed, for the time being, to lift their restrictions on the timing and content of BBC news bulletins. News was broadcast at 1 p.m., 4 p.m., 7 p.m. and 9.30 p.m., more often than not read by Hibberd. The calm way in which bulletins were written and read, in marked contrast to the flamboyant tone of the *British Gazette*, did much to steady the mood of the country. The BBC, as Reith expressed it, was 'for the Government in the crisis'. Nevertheless his refusal to allow Churchill to mobilise the forces of broadcasting as an all-out propaganda weapon against the strikers provoked a serious split in the Cabinet strike committee.

Reith had prepared a statement defending the BBC's attitude which he intended to broadcast himself after the 1 p.m. news on 12 May. Hibberd crept into the studio with a piece of tape that had just come in and passed it to the Managing Director. Reith wrote on it: 'Get this confirmed from No 10 Downing Street.' Hibberd returned shortly with the confirmation and Reith announced that the strike was over.

Broadcasting's stance in a divided nation helped towards the conversion of the private company into a public corporation operating under a Royal Charter. This came into effect on 1 January 1927, with Reith, at the age of 37, being given a knighthood, and his title changed from Managing Director to Director-General.

Stuart Hibberd's best-remembered announcement is his reading of the bulletin issued by King George V's physicians on 20 January 1936: 'The King's life is moving peacefully towards its close.' Every quarter of an hour throughout the evening, following the chimes of Big Ben, he repeated the sentence, until at midnight Sir John Reith announced the Monarch's death. We now know that Lord Dawson of Penn, the physician-in-ordinary, had injected the dose of morphine that had actually moved the King's life to its close. He had also arranged the release of the announcement so that it would catch the first edition of *The Times* rather than the evening newspapers.

In 1992 Buckingham Palace settled the controversy about the King's valedictory words. A widely held version was that he complained to his doctor: 'Dawson, I feel dreadful.' Lord Dawson reassured King George that he was getting better and would soon be sent back to Bognor Regis to recuperate. 'Bugger Bognor,' said the King, and died. It was officially given out that His Majesty's last words were: 'How is the Empire?' Over half a century later, in response to an inquiry from the Mayor of Bognor Regis, the Palace confirmed that the popular version was probably correct.

During the war the chief announcer began to falter. W. E. Williams, writing in *The Listener* in 1943, declared, 'Stuart Hibberd has a voice and a manner which seem to rouse violent partisanship among listeners. He frequently misses his footing as he delivers a bulletin, as though he didn't quite know what a passage meant.' However, his very sympathetic voice retained for him the affection of most of his listeners, especially from 1949 onwards when he regularly presented *The Silver Lining*.

The Silver Lining was a radio programme broadcast on Thursday afternoons, which was designed to bring comfort to people who were housebound or disabled. It matched Hibberd's own strong Christian faith. When fatigue finally got the better of him in 1951 and he retired to the West Country, he continued to introduce *The Silver Lining*, putting himself on the air from an unattended studio in Exeter every week until the programme came to an end in 1964. He was a courteous, reticent man, much liked by those of us who worked with him.

3

John Snagge

'I don't know who is ahead. It is either Oxford or Cambridge.'

John Derrick Mordaunt Snagge, OBE, born 8 May 1904, married 1st 1936 Eileen Mary Joscelyne (died 1980), 2nd 1983 Joan Mary Wilson (died 1992); joined BBC 1924, Assistant Station Director, Stoke-on-Trent 1924, Announcer, Savoy Hill 1928, Assistant, Outside Broadcasts Department 1933, commentator, Oxford and Cambridge Boat Race 1931–80, Assistant Director, Outside Broadcasts 1939, Presentation Director 1939–45, Head of Presentation (Home Service) 1945–57, Head of Presentation (Sound) 1957–63, Special Duties 1963–65; chairman, president, secretary and trustee of the Lord's Taverners.

Reith's intake into the young British Broadcasting Company was by no means limited to ex-servicemen. Many young graduates seeking their first employment were attracted to broadcasting. One of these was John Snagge whose voice was to become one of the best known in the land.

Snagge had been educated at Winchester and Pembroke College, Oxford. He had rowed for his college, but not for the university. In 1924 he came down from Oxford, at the age of 20, with no specialist qualifications other than his record as an oarsman and a fine resonant voice. He sent an application to the BBC, but received no reply.

John's father, Sir Mordaunt Snagge, who was a formidable judge, decided to find out why. He called at Savoy Hill, without an appointment, and demanded to see Reith, who happened to be out. The commissionaire was about to send him away when Sir Mordaunt produced his card. He was immediately shown in to see Reith's deputy, Admiral Charles Carpendale. 'Carps', as he was generally known in the BBC, apologised for the failure to reply and explained that the two-year-old company had been deluged with applications for jobs in broadcasting. He was having to go through fifteen hundred of them. 'I am not interested in the other fourteen hundred and ninety-nine,' said Sir Mordaunt magisterially. John got his interview and in December 1924 was appointed as the Assistant Director of the local radio station which had been established two months earlier at Stoke-on-Trent. His salary was £5 a week.

The main function of the Stoke station was to relay programmes from London. In addition it broadcast local news, supplied by the *Staffordshire Sentinel*, and, on Wednesday evenings, a programme of local talent, including music and talks. Every day Stoke had its own programme for children. Neither the Station Director, Joseph Clarke, nor Snagge had had any programme experience. They just had to invent what to do. Clarke was 'Uncle Joe' and Snagge became 'Uncle Tom' – John being too similar to Joe.

The listeners in those days were also new to broadcasting, and reactions were varied. One lady complained about the BBC's effrontery in broadcasting to her when she was in her bath. Another thought it relevant to inform the station that she kept her wearing apparel in a pineapple basket (whatever that may be) underneath her bed. The General Strike greatly increased local interest in the BBC, and Clarke and Snagge decided to open their single studio for listeners to come and see it for themselves. The studio was ventilated by two large, slowly rotating ceiling fans. One visitor said: 'Ah now I see how the wireless works. You blow the programmes out.'

At Stoke Snagge learned many of the arts of broadcasting, but not the one for which he was to become principally renowned: the running commentary on an event such as the Oxford and Cambridge Boat Race. Reith had tried in 1925 to abolish the restrictions against covering sports events that had been imposed on the company by the press interests. He proposed that what was called a 'coded narrative' of the Boat Race, as well as of the Derby, the Cup Final and the England–Scotland rugger match, should be allowed to be transmitted. However, the press lords would have none of it, and the Post Office failed to arbitrate in the BBC's favour.

In 1927 the British Broadcasting *Corporation* under Royal Charter had supplanted the old limited company, and with the change came greater freedom to broadcast controversial subjects and to cover the main sporting events. The Cup Final, Wimbledon, the Grand National, international rugby and cricket test matches were all broadcast on radio for the first time, and so was the Putney to Mortlake Boat Race between Oxford and Cambridge. The first commentators in the launch following the crews were Oliver Nickalls and the well-known parodist J. C. Squire. Snagge himself broadcast his first sports commentary in January 1927, when Stoke City played Hull City at soccer.

The opening of the powerful transmitter at Daventry in 1928 removed the need for local relay stations. Stoke and the other small ones were closed down and Snagge was transferred to London to join Stuart Hibberd as one of the main announcers. He was soon moved to the new Outside Broadcasts Department. In 1931 he gave the Boat Race commentary, the first of a series which spanned almost half a century, always on radio, eschewing television. Many who had little direct interest in Oxbridge were caught up in the excitement which Snagge's description conveyed. His commentaries were also broadcast by shortwave overseas.

Sometimes there were untoward incidents. One year Eric Maschwitz accompanied Snagge as the second commentator. Although he had memorised various landmarks along the course he gave such an inaccurate performance that Snagge himself began to miscount the strokes. The BBC received a cable from an officers' mess in the Sudan complaining that the whole broadcast had been a scandal. Another year, much later, the engine of the television launch broke down, and poor Snagge was reduced to saying 'I don't know who is ahead. It is either Oxford or Cambridge' – a lapse which was to dog him for many years.

Before each Boat Race the presidents of the Oxford and Cambridge rowing clubs use a gold sovereign presented by John Snagge to toss for the choice of the Middlesex or Surrey station. It is dated 1829, the year the race was started. Snagge searched for the coin for a long time before finally finding it in a shop in Great Portland Street, round the corner from Broadcasting House. He suggested that it should be held between the races by the winning president, but the Amateur Rowing Association said this was impossible. It would mean that the race was being rowed for money, for an 1829 sovereign is still legal tender. Then someone had the bright idea that the coin should be kept by the losing president, so that the race was actually being run to lose money. As Snagge said, 'You can't get more amateur than that.'

Snagge was a most versatile commentator. When the new 80,000-ton liner *Queen Mary* made her maiden voyage across the Atlantic in May 1936 he described the trip in the first series of ship-to-shore broadcasts to be publicly transmitted. He also took part in the start of the world's first high-definition television service in November 1936 at Alexandra Palace where he interviewed the King's Bargemaster, 'Bossy' Phelps.

In 1937 Snagge was waiting to describe the Spithead Review of the Fleet when Princess Elizabeth, then nearly 11, spotted the Outside Broadcasts van and urged her parents to come and look at it. King George VI questioned Snagge at length about the technique of commentary work, and gave him many details about the ceremony to come, which were later used to advantage. The same year, from a position opposite Buckingham Palace, Snagge gave the commentary on the start of the Coronation procession and on its return many hours later.

On the outbreak of war, Snagge became Presentation Director, responsible for all the announcing staff. He decided that the names of the previously anonymous announcers should be given. His real concern was the morale of his staff. It seemed unfair that an announcer's name should be publicised when he was giving a sports commentary but not when he was making presentation announcements or reading the news. When questioned, however, Snagge declared it was for security reasons. The Nazis were known to be training speakers to imitate BBC voices, and in wartime security was an unchallengeable justification.

Snagge broadcast many of the important wartime

announcements himself, including the first communiqué from the Supreme Headquarters, Allied Expeditionary Force, telling of the D-Day landings in France. Originally SHAEF had planned that the announcement should be made by two voices, the first being General Eisenhower's military correspondent Colonel Dupuis. W. J. Haley, the new BBC Director-General, declared that the use of an American voice first would cause confusion, and insisted that it must be one of the BBC's regular named announcers. Later that same day Snagge introduced the first edition of *War Report*, a news magazine of actuality material from the beachhead which daily gave vivid accounts of the progress of the liberation of Europe to audiences of from ten to fifteen million people. His words 'and now over to Normandy' were long remembered.

The return of peace brought the return of the Boat Race and re-established Snagge as the supreme commentator for this event. He also became one of the principal commentators for State occasions for radio, as Richard Dimbleby became for television. For the Queen's Coronation in 1953 he gave the commentary from the triforium in Westminster Abbey.

At that time, before satellite communication, the closest that America's breakfast television programme *Today* could get to live coverage of the Coronation ceremony was to relay sound of the World Service, with Snagge's commentary, while punching up still pictures to illustrate what he was saying. When the shortwave reception faltered, as it unfortunately did during one of the more solemn moments in the Abbey, *Today* faded out John Snagge and went into a tasteless interview with one of the programme's regular ingredients, a chimpanzee called J. Fred Muggs, who was asked whether they had coronations in his chimpland. Some British newspapers played up the incident as an awful warning of what to expect when commercial television, newly authorised by the government, started in Britain.

Snagge retired in 1965 but continued to give the television commentaries on the Boat Race. Three years later *Dad's Army* began its droll portrayal of the Home Guard in wartime. The events of a quarter of a century earlier were remembered by many, but the post-war generation needed to have the scene set for them, and what voice was more suitable than that of the man who had introduced *War Report*? However, the style in which those prefaces to *Dad's Army* were written was closer to the chauvinistic tone of the wartime cinema newsreels than to the way the BBC had reported the war. Snagge also broadcast regularly for Radio London after the BBC re-established the local stations which had given him his start in broadcasting half a century earlier.

John Snagge and his wife Eileen lived in a Buckinghamshire house with a large garden close to the Stoke Poges country churchyard immortalised by Gray's 'Elegy'. In 1979 they thought it was time to move to somewhere that was easier to keep up. They managed to sell their house immediately and found what seemed to be an ideal new home in Dorney, a village with a fine view of nearby Windsor Castle. It had a good general store, was right on a bus route, and perhaps it did not matter that they had no roots in Dorney and knew virtually no one there.

By a sad turn of fate, within six months the general store had been closed, the bus route had been discontinued, and Eileen Snagge had died. After the funeral at Gray's church in Stoke Poges John became a rather pitiful figure. His health had begun to deteriorate. He lacked the support of familiar neighbours. Without children to comfort him he was lonely. Then fate took another and better twist. In 1982 the Variety Club of Great Britain gave a lunch in honour of the BBC's sixtieth anniversary. John found himself sitting next to a former BBC colleague, Joan Wilson. A few months later they were married and the next nine years were happy ones for John Snagge. Then, when he was 88, she also died.

It is a mistake to think of John Snagge merely as the resonant voice of Boat Races and other sports. He is a man of deep emotions. Reflecting on the Queen's Coronation in 1953 he once said:

'When it came to the real thing, the true, live ceremony, with the golden carpet, the blue brocade – when you saw the royals come in, when you saw the peers in their full robes, and the crowned Heads of State, when you saw the whole ceremony, mounting in traditional rite and splendour to its incredible climax of colour and sound – when you saw all this from the supreme vantage-point, in all its detail – *that* was the test, to do a professional job under the strain of your own deep personal emotion. Whether the emotion you felt was conveyed to the listener, I wouldn't know. It must have had some effect, even though there were times when you experienced difficulty in speaking at all. You're on your own, it's up to you – and the best of luck, chum!'

4

Eric Maschwitz

'These Foolish Things'

*Albert Eric Maschwitz, OBE 1937, born Birmingham 10 June
1901, married 1st 1926 Hermione Gingold, 2nd 1945 Phyllis
Gordon; edited group of Hutchinson's magazines 1922–23,
joined BBC 1926, Editor,* Radio Times *1927–33, Director
of Variety 1933–37, MGM Hollywood 1937–38; Intelligence
Corps 1940–42, inaugurated Army Broadcasting Section, War
Office 1942, Lieutenant-Colonel in charge of Broadcasting, 21
Army Group 1945; Head of Light Entertainment, Television,
BBC 1958–61; Assistant and Adviser to Controller of Tele-
vision Programmes, BBC 1961–63; director of the Performing
Right Society; producer (special projects), Rediffusion Tele-
vision 1963; died 27 October 1969, aged 68.*

There was considerable surprise in the television service
in 1958 at the news that Eric Maschwitz was returning to
the BBC as Head of Light Entertainment. He had been
away from it for twenty-one years and was 57; some
feared he might be a rather old dog to learn new tricks.
He had gained a high reputation in the world of show
business as the creator and producer of famous musical
plays and revues. He had written several successful
novels and the lyrics of evergreen songs, such as 'These

Foolish Things', 'A Nightingale Sang in Berkeley Square' and 'Room 504'. But how good would he be in the world of television light entertainment? He soon showed that he would be excellent.

Maschwitz himself disliked the term 'light entertainment'. 'What is its alternative?' he would scornfully ask. 'Heavy entertainment? Or perhaps dark entertainment?' His comparable job in radio in the 1930s had been called Director of Variety. He and his colleague Val Gielgud, the Director of Drama, at that time shared responsibility for the third element of Reith's concept of the BBC's programme obligations: entertainment (as well as information and education).

Eric Maschwitz and Val Gielgud, an elder brother of Sir John, were both descended from Polish military families, and were collectively known in the BBC as the Polish Corridor. Maschwitz's grandfather had emigrated to Birmingham in the middle of the nineteenth century. When *The Black and White Minstrel Show*, which Eric had started, won the Golden Rose trophy at the Montreux Festival in 1961, he liked to recount that the representatives of the British Broadcasting Corporation there bore the somewhat un-British names of Maschwitz, Djurkovitch, Levin and Dorfman.

Eric Maschwitz entered Repton as a classical scholar in 1915 and four years later went up to Gonville and Caius College, Cambridge, with a scholarship in Modern Languages. Much of his time at the university was spent in acting and journalism. One of his closest friends there was Lance Sieveking, the tall, good-looking godson of G. K. Chesterton. He was later to become a pioneer of radio drama and the producer of the very first televised play, adapted from Pirandello's *The Man with the Flower in his Mouth*. It was shown on John Logie Baird's experimental

30-line television service in Long Acre in 1930.

After Cambridge Maschwitz worked for a year in magazine publishing and then lived a rickety Bohemian life as an impecunious freelance writer. He was tall – well over 6 feet – handsome, and by nature a Lothario. He produced a bestselling novel *A Taste of Honey* shortly before he married Hermione Gingold, the actress with the roguish smile and the elegant legs who later became the star of sophisticated revue. Much later she starred in the film *Gigi* and with Maurice Chevalier memorably recorded 'I Remember it Well'.

At the time of the General Strike of 1926, however, they were again penniless. Eric had been working as a special constable, as he recorded in his entertaining autobiography *No Chip on My Shoulder*, 'more to fill the empty days with a little adventure than with the idea of opposing the workers of the world'. Shortly after the strike had ended he ran into his Cambridge friend Lance Sieveking who, hearing he needed a job, introduced him to Admiral Charles Carpendale. Maschwitz was offered an appointment in the outside broadcasting department at Savoy Hill.

The *Radio Times*, then three years old, was also edited at Savoy Hill. At that time its weekly circulation was less than half a million copies and its bookish editor was a far from practical organiser. After a few months working on outside broadcasts, Maschwitz, on the strength of his magazine publishing experience, was appointed 'Managing Editor' to give him support. After the Editor's sudden death from a heart attack a few weeks later, Maschwitz, then 26, became the new Editor of the *Radio Times*.

For the next seven years Eric Maschwitz built the magazine into a highly successful enterprise. He recruited various talented assistants who went on to higher things within the Corporation. One was Val Gielgud who was soon promoted from the Listeners' Letters page to become Director of Productions. This move followed Gielgud's skilful direction of a BBC staff amateur dramatic show in which Reith gave a surprisingly comic performance as a drunken broker's man. Another recruit was Laurence Gilliam, later the Head of Features who created the elaborate Christmas Day radio programmes that led up to the Monarch's broadcast, and a third was Maurice Gorham, who succeeded Maschwitz as Editor of the *Radio Times* and went on to become Director of the Forces Programme and Head of Television.

The *Radio Times* was not merely a programme schedule. It commissioned articles from many of the leading writers of the day, such as Sacheverell Sitwell and Compton Mackenzie. With the support of a strong editorial team Maschwitz found he had enough spare time in the evenings to take up creative writing again.

One of his first ventures, at Gielgud's behest, was to convert Compton Mackenzie's novel *Carnival* into a complicated radio play with a hundred scenes. It ran for over two hours, involved two orchestras, and used all the Savoy Hill studios linked together. *Carnival* was very popular and rebroadcast many times. In 1932 Gielgud wanted to mount a radio operetta using the same techniques. A contemporary of Maschwitz at Repton and Cambridge introduced him to George Posford, a young musician who had written some tuneful melodies and was looking for a librettist. Eric, using the pen-name Holt Marvell, obliged by writing *Good Night Vienna*, which he said included almost every sugary cliché imaginable.

The day after *Good Night Vienna* was broadcast Herbert Wilcox bought the film rights to make the first British musical talkie, starring his wife Anna Neagle and Jack

Buchanan. The film ran for fourteen consecutive weeks in London and the stage version has often been revived. One of these revivals, identified by Donald Sinden after much painstaking research, was in March 1948 at the Lewisham Hippodrome. Eric Maschwitz, who loved to tell stories against himself, recounted to all and sundry how he went there one rainy evening and saw the stage manager sheltering under a canopy. Sidling up to him, and without revealing that he was Holt Marvell, Eric asked how it was doing. 'Just about as well as "Good Night Lewisham" would do in Vienna' was the lugubrious reply.

By 1933, the year after the BBC moved from Savoy Hill to the custom-built Broadcasting House, Val Gielgud had more work in the Productions Department than he cared for. He wanted to concentrate on radio drama 'without troubling himself with ukulele players and comedians', as a colleague put it. A separate Variety Department was created and Eric Maschwitz was made its Director.

The four years he held that post were vintage ones for British popular music. Noel Coward, Vivian Ellis, Ray Noble, George Posford and Jack Strachey were writing the songs that people sang and still sing. Cole Porter's 'You're the Top' in *Anything Goes* encouraged Eric to try his hand at a catalogue song on a romantic theme. The result was 'These Foolish Things', with music by Jack Strachey. At first it aroused little interest. Then Leslie Hutchinson – 'Hutch', the popular West Indian singer – took a fancy to it and made a record. When we were working together in the 1960s Eric told me he was still making £1,000 a year in royalties from his memories of young love – and of a pre-war rate of exchange:

> Gardenia perfume ling'ring on a pillow
> Wild strawberries only seven francs a kilo

And still my heart has wings
These Foolish Things remind me of you ...

Maschwitz broadcast productions of *Bitter Sweet*, *The Student Prince* and *The Vagabond King* as well as programmes starring Eddie Cantor and the Boswell Sisters. For regular performances he also had Henry Hall and the Dance Orchestra, the Kentucky Minstrels and Reginald Foort on the theatre organ.

He also started a new BBC theatre in St George's Hall, across Langham Place from Broadcasting House, which became the headquarters of variety. From there he introduced a raft of new entertainment programmes, the first of which was the interview show *In Town Tonight*. Maschwitz himself chose its famous signature tune, Eric Coates's 'Knightsbridge March'. Another popular series was *Scrapbook*, written by Leslie Baily, which recalled in a lively manner the events of a particular year. Occasionally he performed as an Outside Broadcasts commentator, as for instance at the Silver Jubilee Ball in the Albert Hall in 1935.

He continued to write prodigiously. With Val Gielgud he co-authored several thrillers, again using the name Holt Marvell. With George Posford he also converted his earlier play *The Gay Hussar* into an improved musical version *Balalaika*, which ran for a year and a half in London, and also opened in Paris, Prague, Stockholm and Sydney.

In 1937, when Maschwitz went to Buckingham Palace to receive the OBE, King George VI recalled that they used to play tennis together at Cambridge. On his return from the Palace he learned that Metro-Goldwyn-Mayer had made a huge offer for the film rights to *Balalaika*. The BBC gave him four weeks leave and he went to

Hollywood to negotiate terms. Michael Balcon, then an executive producer with MGM, persuaded him to accept a writing contract worth ten times his BBC salary. He submitted his resignation, believing he was giving up a broadcasting career for ever.

Hollywood provided Maschwitz with a luxurious life and a chance to make many friends but gave him virtually nothing to do. He was about to return to England when he was asked to look at the script of *Goodbye, Mr Chips*, which had been adapted by R. C. Sherriff, the author of *Journey's End*, from James Hilton's novel. Maschwitz made vast improvements to Sherriff's version, and persuaded the director to use Repton as the location for Mr Chips's school. He even wrote a school song for it, and the result was a highly successful film.

Eric Maschwitz's next song was 'A Nightingale Sang in Berkeley Square'. He wrote it just before the war. Peter Dimmock remembers him in late 1939 sitting down at the piano and trying it out at The Gay Nineties, a night-club just off Berkeley Square run by Phyllis Gordon, a very pretty girl with auburn hair. Dimmock admits he did not think very much of the song at the time, but it was an immediate hit in April 1940 when Judy Campbell launched it in the sophisticated wartime revue *New Faces*.

Maschwitz managed to produce *New Faces* in his spare time while employed by the Postal Censorship. During the Second World War he held a variety of different jobs, some in uniform, some not. As Deputy Assistant Director of Army Welfare involved in the distribution of wireless sets to the troops he wore a major's crown on his shoulder. Transferred to the Special Operations Executive and flown to America before Pearl Harbor to join British Security

Coordination in New York, he was given a passport describing his profession as 'Ministry of Supply'. He was supposed to be a former playwright on war work as a civilian. In fact he was helping to keep an eye on enemy forces at work in a neutral country.

Other wartime jobs included preparing propaganda leaflets for the Political Warfare Executive at its secret headquarters in Woburn Abbey and working with Peter Ustinov in the film unit of General Eisenhower's Supreme Headquarters, Allied Expeditionary Force, on the movie about the liberation of Europe, *The True Glory*.

At the end of the war he returned to radio and was involved in setting up what became the British Forces Network in Germany. He had been divorced from Hermione Gingold and, as soon as he was demobilised, married Phyllis Gordon of The Gay Nineties.

Renewing his partnership with Jack Strachey, who composed the music for 'These Foolish Things', he wrote a musical play, *Belinda Fair*, for Adele Dixon, an attractive singer who had introduced television at Alexandra Palace on its opening day in November 1936. He also started writing for television himself. First was a weekly series of comedies called *Family Affairs*. Then came a television adaptation of his 90-minute play *Carissima* starring Barbara Kelly, which required the use of both the small studios at Alexandra Palace with complicated re-setting of scenery in the studio temporarily not being used. There was no videotaping at that time, and all plays were transmitted live.

When Eric Maschwitz, with his wealth of show business experience, became responsible for television Light Entertainment in 1958 those two small studios had been replaced by four much larger ones at Lime Grove and the Television Theatre at Shepherd's Bush. Soon there would be many even larger ones at Television Centre, which he would exploit to the full.

BBC Light Entertainment under his leadership flourished as never before. *The Black and White Minstrel Show,* one of his first new programmes, was for long a favourite for its tuneful music, its pretty girls and its stylish dancing, though eventually there were complaints that it demeaned black people. *Juke Box Jury* was popular with the younger set. Comedy shows such as *Hancock's Half-Hour, Steptoe and Son* and *Dad's Army* were popular with everyone. So were *The Charlie Drake Show* and *Whacko,* the story of a crazy schoolmaster starring Jimmy Edwards and written by Frank Muir and Denis Norden.

Maschwitz brought in Muir and Norden as high-level advisers and consultants to the Light Entertainment department. Both of them are splendidly funny as writers, equally so as performers in various broadcast panel games, and particularly so in private conversation. In the elitist days when Television Centre had a senior dining-room (dubbed by Maschwitz the 'Café Sordide') their lunchtime talk kept their colleagues in constant laughter. Muir and Norden jointly received the Screenwriters Guild award for the best contribution to light entertainment in 1961.

In 1961 Maschwitz turned over the day-to-day running of the department to his assistant Tom Sloan, but he remained the Light Entertainment supremo until 1963. By that time Donald Baverstock had been appointed Assistant Controller of Television Programmes, promoted over Maschwitz's head, as well as over the heads of the drama, women's programmes and children's programmes departments, all considerably older than he was. Baverstock had little talent for man-management but plenty of interference, and within a few months all four departmental heads had left the television service. Maschwitz went to Rediffusion Television as a producer of special projects. He was a sad loss to the BBC.

5

Alistair Cooke

*'The best broadcaster on five
continents'*

*Alfred Alistair Cooke, Hon. KBE 1973, journalist, broadcaster
and author, born Salford 20 November 1908, married 1st 1934
Ruth Emerson, one son, 2nd 1946 Jane White Hawkes, one
daughter; BBC film critic 1934–37; London correspondent for
NBC 1936–37; commentator on American affairs BBC from
1938; special correspondent on American affairs,* The Times
1938–40, American feature writer, Daily Herald *1941–43,
UN correspondent,* Manchester Guardian *1945–48, chief cor-
respondent in the US,* Guardian *1948–72; Master of Cer-
emonies,* Omnibus *1961–67,* International Zone *1961–67,
Masterpiece Theater 1971–93; Benjamin Franklin Medal,
RSA; Howland Medal, Yale University; publications: (ed.)*
Garbo and the Night Watchman, *1937,* Douglas Fairbanks:
The Making of a Screen Character *1970,* A Generation on
Trial: USA v Alger Hiss *1950,* Letters from America *1951,*
Christmas Eve *1952,* A Commencement Address *1954,
(ed.)* The Vintage Mencken *1955,* Around the World in
Fifty Years *1966,* Talk about America *1968,* Alistair
Cooke's America *1973,* Six Men *1977,* The Americans:
Fifty Letters from America on our Life and Times *1979,
(with Robert Cameron)* Above London *1980,* Masterpieces
1982, The Patient has the Floor *1986; honorary degrees from*

Edinburgh, Manchester, St Andrews; Honorary Fellow, Jesus College, Cambridge.

Alistair Cooke has been broadcasting for the BBC so regularly and for so long that many assume he must be on its staff. He never has been. The nearest he came to it was when the BBC engaged him on programme contract before the war as its film critic.

It happened thus: in the spring of 1934 Cooke was a 25-year-old English graduate from Cambridge nearing the end of a two-year Commonwealth Fund fellowship in America. It had taken him first to Yale to study theatre direction, and then to Harvard to research into the history of the English language in the United States.

Alistair Cooke, who was a Lancastrian, had won many of the glittering prizes at Cambridge. He had been a scholar of Jesus College, gained a first in the English tripos, edited *The Granta*, and founded the Mummers, an acting club for whose revues he wrote both words and music. He had also been the Cambridge drama critic of *The Nation* and *Athenæum*.

One day he noticed in a Boston paper the startling headline 'BBC Fires Premier's Son', and then read the rather less startling news that the BBC had decided not to renew its programme contract with Oliver Baldwin, the socialist son of Prime Minister Stanley Baldwin, who had been broadcasting a series of weekly radio programmes reviewing what in those days were called the talkies.

Alistair Cooke set his heart on becoming the BBC's new film critic. He sent a cable to Broadcasting House mentioning that he would be working in Hollywood that summer with Charlie Chaplin, and offering to catch the first liner across the Atlantic for an interview if he were a shortlisted candidate for the vacancy. He had first cannily checked with the Commonwealth Fund authorities that they would pay his return fare if he stood a good chance of landing the job.

He landed it easily, and that autumn began the longest professional talking career in the history of broadcasting. Cooke loved movies, and was knowledgeable about them, so the content of his talks was good. There were no tape recorders and very little recording at all in those pre-war years, the heyday of the scripted talk. With the help of skilled BBC producers Alistair soon perfected the technique of informal delivery which concealed the fact that every word was being read from a script that had been carefully composed to be read aloud. Harold Nicolson, another graceful essayist of the airwaves at that time, described Cooke as 'the best broadcaster on five continents'.

Cooke's Commonwealth Fund Fellowship had taken him to America in 1932 when it was in the depths of the Depression and was about to elect Franklin Roosevelt as its next President. The Fund had enabled him to travel widely around the United States. So, in addition to film criticism, Cooke started broadcasting on the BBC about other aspects of American life. One subject was jazz, which he loved and played well on the piano. Between 1974 and 1988 he broadcast more than seventy BBC programmes about American jazz, first on Radio 3, next on Radio 2 and finally on Radio 4.

Another of Cooke's pre-war series concerned the difference between the American and the British forms of English, the subject he had been studying at Harvard. Some of the examples he used in his broadcasts came to the attention of H. L. Mencken, the distinguished author of *The American Language*.

The National Broadcasting Company relayed several of Alistair Cooke's BBC talks in the United States and at one stage engaged him to broadcast a regular *London Letter*. NBC's regular London correspondent, Fred Bate, was a friend of King Edward VIII, but when the story of the King's affair with Mrs Simpson, and the possibility of an abdication, suddenly came into the public domain, Bate had the misfortune to be on leave in the United States.

There was no way then for him to get back to London in under five days, so he telephoned Alistair Cooke and urged him to rush to Broadcasting House and provide a news dispatch for NBC before the midnight circuit already booked by the rival American radio network CBS. Cooke made it, just in time. He had flu and a high temperature, but for the next ten days of the developing abdication crisis he broadcast to America six or seven times a day from a microphone which the Post Office rigged up in his living room. NBC were very grateful for that mammoth stint and appointed him one of their London correspondents.

In 1937 Alistair Cooke emigrated to the United States. When he made his first visit there five years earlier, he had fallen in love with America, and also with a stunning American girl, Ruth Emerson. She was the daughter of the Surgeon-General of the United States and became Cooke's first wife. They had a son, John, who inherited his father's love of jazz and later became a successful author of Western novels. Alistair collaborated with H. L. Mencken on a supplement to his famous lexicon, and also worked as a special correspondent for *The Times*. Later he wrote for the *Daily Herald* and the *Manchester Guardian* and contributed news dispatches to the BBC which at that time had no staff news correspondent in America.

The process of becoming a United States citizen is tediously slow, and by the time Alistair Cooke's naturalisation papers came through Britain was not only at war but very close to defeat. Some people thought he had deliberately chosen that dark moment to renounce his British heritage, and raised stridently critical voices against him. The British Information Services in New York were instructed not to offer him any help. He was officially cold-shouldered.

All that has long since been forgotten and forgiven, most publicly in 1973 when the Queen awarded him an honorary knighthood. But it hurt Alistair at the time, and he has suffered ever since from a problem of national identity. Despite his US citizenship, Americans still think of him as the quintessential Englishman. That is why he was chosen to introduce, for over twenty years, *Masterpiece Theater*, the weekly programme on the American public television network which re-broadcasts the best dramatic serials produced by BBC and ITV. Most British listeners to *Letter from America*, on the other hand, regard him as a particularly urbane American. He is the real mid-Atlantic man.

Cooke's first marriage broke up during the war but he later married Jane White Hawkes, the widowed mother of two young children whose husband had died while on naval service in the Pacific. She is not only an attractive woman but also a talented painter. Their daughter Susan, married and living in New England, features frequently in *Letter from America*, the series started in March 1946.

Originally due to run for thirteen weeks, it has become the longest-running talks series broadcast anywhere. Some have described it as the greatest interpretation of America to the rest of the world since the writings of Alexis de Tocqueville in 1835.

Cooke was at that time employed by the *Manchester Guardian*, first as its United Nations correspondent, later as the chief of its American bureau. I was then the BBC's first peacetime correspondent in America and we frequently covered the same news stories. We sat next to each other throughout the two long, puzzling trials of Alger Hiss, about whom Cooke wrote his book *A Generation on Trial. Letter from America* often drew on his reporting assignments, and in later years on reminiscences of them, but they were never limited to dispatches of straight news. They were perceptive and affectionate interpretations of America's joys, troubles, strengths and weaknesses, written with humour and compassion, and always beautifully delivered.

In May 1952 I attended a ceremonial lunch in New York when Alistair received a Peabody Award for *Letter from America*. Other recipients of these coveted radio and television awards included Ed Murrow for his *See it Now* television series and Gian-Carlo Menotti for the moving opera *Amahl and the Night Visitors*. There were also awards for the stand-up comedians Bob Hope and Jack Benny. However, their gag-writers were not in very good form that day, and their remarks disappointed the American network moguls at the top table.

The last award on the list was for the best contribution to international understanding. Alistair Cooke in those days was not a familiar face, or voice, or even name, to the American public. He made a short but elegant and witty acceptance speech. He ended his remarks, as all the stars of American commercial broadcasting had done, by thanking his sponsor. 'You may wonder who the sponsor is,' he said. 'It is the British people who pay me to bat them over the head once a week by telling them why they are wrong about the Americans.'

Immediately after the lunch several of the network bosses offered Alistair Cooke television contracts. He became the anchorman of *Omnibus*, a cultural magazine carried by the American Broadcasting Company's network, sponsored by the Ford Foundation. It was a good programme which lasted for nine years and Alistair became a well-known personality on American television – what Hollywood used to call 'flesh'.

In 1957, when Alistair Cooke's friend Nunnally Johnson was producing and directing his 'faction' cinema film *The Three Faces of Eve* about a multiple personality, he needed 'flesh' to explain that Eve White's story really did happen, although she was being played by the actress Joanne Woodward. He invited Alistair to speak a short foreword, guaranteeing, as it were, the truth, the whole truth and nothing but the truth of the film.

Cooke was delighted to take part, particularly because it would give him a chance to revisit California without having to ask the *Guardian* for the fare. The Hollywood studio telephoned, querying whether they should discuss the fee with him or with his agent. Cooke said he would get his agent to ring back and immediately sought advice about agents. He was recommended to contact Irving Kohn, not actually an agent but a lawyer and a very skilful tax expert.

Cooke told Kohn that the work of recording the short introduction could not possibly take him more than one morning, but he would like the studio to pay for his wife Jane to fly to Los Angeles with him, arrange a car to meet them, and put them up in a Hollywood hotel for a fortnight. If there was a small honorarium so much the better. But the important points were Jane's fare, the car, and the hotel for a fortnight.

Kohn rang the studio and in no time arranged first class

air passages for Jane and Alistair, the car, and a three-week stay in an airconditioned suite in the Beverly Hills Hilton. Then came the matter of the honorarium. Alistair on his own would have gladly settled for something like $250. To his horror he heard Irving Kohn say, 'Two thousand dollars? Why Mr Cooke wouldn't go to Hoboken for two thousand dollars' – Hoboken being just across the Hudson river from New York City. 'A foreign correspondent of Mr Cooke's status would not leave his post for a penny less than ten thousand dollars.' The studio settled immediately. That is why you employ a lawyer such as Irving Kohn.

Kohn also negotiated the sale of the rights to the book derived from his television documentary series *America*. It sold 1.2 million copies in the United States, as well as half a million in the United Kingdom, and made Alistair a very rich man. *America*, written and presented by Alistair, explored the pageant of American history in thirteen segments. It was commissioned by Stephen Hearst and produced by Michael Gill. It followed in the line of BBC2 television blockbusters pioneered by Kenneth Clark's *Civilisation* and Jacob Bronowski's *The Ascent of Man*. The *America* series won another Peabody and four Emmys. It also gained for Cooke the Richard Dimbleby BAFTA award and the Benjamin Franklin award of the Royal Society of Arts. It was shown throughout the United States on the NBC network and in thirty other countries around the world. The MacArthur Foundation presented videotape copies of it to every public library in America.

America was prepared in celebration of the bicentennial of the United States. One of Alistair Cooke's many honours was to be invited, on 25 September 1974, to address the United States House of Representatives in commemoration of the 200th anniversary of the first Continental Congress. The *Guardian* in a leader the next day described it as 'a mighty compliment to journalism, to the world of letters, and above all to the man himself that the Congress of the United States should want to learn from the good reporter Cooke'. It added: 'The BBC for whom he has reported America since 1937, and the *Guardian*, for whom he has been writing since 1945, will both feel warmed by a shaft or two of reflected glory.'

Alistair and Jane Cooke live in a New York apartment overlooking Central Park. It has many Staffordshire figures, which Alistair collects with pleasure, and masses of books. They also have a house on Long Island where they relax in the summer, Jane to paint and Alistair to play golf, a game he took up late in life. Like a religious convert he has desperately been making up for lost time. They also make frequent visits to London and to San Francisco, which is where Alistair would really like to live.

Now in his mid-eighties, Alistair Cooke has relinquished most of his regular broadcasting commitments except his weekly radio *Letter from America*, which has run since early in 1946. On St Valentine's Day that year he proposed the idea, describing it as 'a weekly personal letter to a Briton by a fireside about American life, and people and places in the American news'. He suggested that the BBC should broadcast it on Sundays 'indefinitely'. After the BBC had cautiously limited the initial series to thirteen, *Letter from America* has indeed continued indefinitely, becoming the longest-running talks series broadcast anywhere in the world.

6

Richard Dimbleby

'He gave warmth to the spoken word,
friendliness to the formal occasion,
and tradition and dignity to the whole
new world of broadcasting.'

Frederick Richard Dimbleby, CBE 1959, OBE 1945, broad-caster, author, newspaper director, editor and film producer, born 25 May 1913, married 1937 Dilys Thomas, three sons one daughter; journalism 1931–36; BBC News Observer 1936, first war correspondent 1939, chief correspondent in Middle East 1940, first BBC correspondent in Berlin during and after Potsdam Conference; resigned from BBC staff 1946 but con-tinued as freelance commentator for major royal, State and governmental occasions, regular radio programmes Down Your Way, Twenty Questions, *television programmes* London Town, About Britain, At Home, Panorama, Choice, Passport; *Honorary LL.D. Sheffield University; died 22 December 1965, aged 52.*

Richard Dimbleby's place as Britain's foremost broad-caster remains unchallenged two generations after his first appearance at the microphone. He was our eye-witness at virtually every momentous event of the mid-twentieth century from the Spanish Civil War to the funeral of Sir Winston Churchill. His death in 1965 was mourned nationally.

He made history as well as observing it. He stimulated the development of news and current affairs broadcasting. In the BBC he was the first news reporter, the first war correspondent, the first commentator for television coverage of a Coronation and of a State Opening of Parliament. He was there each time television significantly extended its range – across the Channel in 1950, through the Iron Curtain in 1961, across the Atlantic by satellite in 1962 and around the world in 1964.

After leaving Mill Hill School Richard Dimbleby went to work in the family local newspaper and printing business in Richmond. He had five years of journalistic apprenticeship, which included reporting for Southern Newspapers in Southampton and becoming the news editor of the *Advertiser's Weekly* in Fleet Street. He then successfully persuaded BBC News to make him its first so-called News Observer. He was 23 and was nicknamed Bumble, because he was large and he buzzed. He had charm and immense self-confidence.

He also had flair and great technical ingenuity. He devised imaginative ways to use radio for eyewitness accounts of all manner of events, both at home and abroad. For instance, during the great Fenland floods of March 1937 he would record onto discs vivid eyewitness accounts and the sounds of the work going on. He would then entrust the discs to the guard of a London-bound train, telephoning the news room to arrange to meet it. He was fascinated by recording, a technique not hitherto used in the BBC news bulletins which were compiled entirely from agency tapes. He had a clear rule that there must be no faking. The bark of a dog that roused the household against a burglar had to be *the* bark of *the* dog, not just the bark of another dog of the same kind. When covering the story of a record-breaking new railway engine he spent much of the journey recording the real sound of the train's wheels by dangling a microphone down a lavatory pan.

I first met Richard in Broadcasting House in the spring of 1939. He was about to leave for Canada and the United States to cover the tour of King George VI and Queen Elizabeth, the first Royal Tour to include a BBC correspondent. I was using his scripts, in translation, as news talks for our broadcasts to Germany, and it was interesting to watch his style mature, and his national reputation grow, during that Royal Tour.

The day that Britain declared war on Germany Dimbleby donned uniform as the BBC's first war correspondent. He found the phoney war in France a frustrating period, and was moved to the Middle East before the German blitz against the British Expeditionary Force. In Egypt and Libya, however, he saw plenty of action. He entered Bardia with the British troops and told how Italian officers and men offered to surrender to him. He went south to Khartoum and was on his way to Abyssinia when he was struck down with diphtheria. He had to spend a month lying on his back, isolated from the world except for a nurse.

Dimbleby covered fighting in Greece and Albania, and a surrender in Syria. He lived cheek by jowl with Nazi intelligence agents in Turkey and was ambushed in Iran by guerrillas. He travelled 100,000 miles in over a dozen countries.

Back in Europe in 1943 he became the BBC's air correspondent, attached to Bomber Command. His first mission was a raid on Berlin in a Lancaster bomber piloted by Guy Gibson. In the next fifteen months he took part in similar raids flying deep into hostile territory. At the same time he was centrally involved in the creation of the War

Reporting Unit which covered the gruelling last year of the war from D-Day to the final collapse of Nazi Germany.

He reported the crossing of the Rhine, was the first war correspondent from the West to enter the ruined German capital, and broadcast from the chair in Hitler's bombed-out study. Shortly before he had given the first eyewitness account of Belsen concentration camp, perhaps the most moving dispatch of his life. His respect for the stability of established procedures and the security of an evolving history dated from that rending experience. He had seen what could happen when human order disintegrated.

I remember pacing along a corridor in Broadcasting House with Richard Dimbleby in the summer of 1945. I had just returned from reporting the immediate post-war situation in Czechoslovakia and was waiting to go out to Washington. Richard was just back from Berlin. He was then earning £1,000 a year and was determined to get £1,100. That day the Administrative Officer in the News Division had refused his request for upgrading as a reporter. If he left the microphone and took an editorial job his ceiling could be raised. Richard was adamant that he was not leaving the microphone. He told me that with the family newspapers behind him he was going to resign from the staff and chance his arm as a freelance broadcaster. For the News Division it was short-sighted parsimony. As a part-time freelance, Richard Dimbleby at the microphone was going to earn far more than £1,100 from the BBC every year for the rest of his life.

At first there were only slim pickings from television – less than £146 in the two years 1946–47. But Richard was sustained, as throughout his broadcasting career, by his most fortunate marriage to Dilys Thomas, the busy mother of his four children. When he left the BBC staff she became his manager, his agent and his most trusted critic.

His versatile early freelance work included being a regular panellist on *Twenty Questions* and travelling over the country to interview people, always courteously, for *Down Your Way* on radio and for *London Town* and *About Britain* on television. Meanwhile he also became the principal BBC commentator for State ceremonies. At occasions ranging from the solemnity of the Lying-in-State of King George VI to the splendour of Queen Elizabeth's Coronation, Dimbleby found felicitous words to bring the scene to life for listeners or to annotate it and add its colour for viewers of black and white television.

In addition to these programmes produced by Peter Dimmock's Outside Broadcasts Department Richard Dimbleby broadcast regularly for Television Talks, the department I headed after my return from Washington. He was the anchorman for *Panorama* on Monday evenings for most of the year, as well as for the General Election results programmes, those exhausting marathons where his meticulous homework, his respect for factual accuracy and his extraordinary stamina served him well.

The reconstructed old film studio at Lime Grove near Shepherd's Bush Green (see Haley, p. 86) seemed to acquire a special air of excitement on *Panorama* nights. There was usually a knot of young people with autograph books outside the main entrance, on the lookout for visitors whose names were in that day's headlines, or would be in the morrow's. Much of *Panorama*'s content in those days came live from the studio, and viewers never knew what to expect. One day it was a French girl of 9, Minou Drouet, who at the beginning of the programme was set the task of composing a poem about London. She was seen writing hard for a while. She got up, bounced a ball once or twice, and resumed her writing. At the end of *Panorama* Dimbleby put his excellent French to use by translating the charming verse she had produced.

Richard Dimbleby had a total mastery of the complicated technique of television presentation. For instance, a film sequence needs to run for eight seconds on a telecine machine, before it reaches full speed. Richard would finger his spectacles, indicating to the studio director the start of his eight-second cue, and would finish his sentence exactly as the first frame came up. His long apprenticeship in radio had made him a master at reading a prepared commentary to a film sequence, and he could complete a last-minute session at the Lime Grove dubbing theatre faster than most, for his readings were always right first time.

Dimbleby's authority was such that he almost acted as a national Ombudsman. His bulky form and his imperturbability provided welcome reassurance. During the Cuban missile crisis, when it looked as though the world was on the brink of nuclear war, and *Panorama* mounted a special programme, a woman telephoned to say that she would only send her children to school if Richard Dimbleby said it was safe to do so.

He was invariably an excellent host and *Panorama*'s guests were always anxious to meet him. One was King Hussein of Jordan who dined with us one night at Lime Grove because he wanted to see television in action. Jordan had not yet started a TV service. We took him on a tour of the studios and finally ended up with *Panorama*, where a memorable interview took place, with the Sandhurst-trained King and the deferential Dimbleby, like Johnson and Boswell, each calling the other 'Sir' in every sentence.

*

Richard's home life at a farm in Surrey, where his three sons and his daughter Sally grew up, was a particularly happy one. He was a delightful companion, with a talent for playing the piano and a lively sense of humour. He resented critics calling him pompous and complaining that on ceremonial occasions he was wont to talk in reverential whispers. He used to have to remind them that the commentator at a solemn ceremony in a large hushed hall had to whisper or he would seriously disrupt the proceedings.

The television broadcast of the funeral of Sir Winston Churchill on 30 January 1965 will be long remembered by those who saw it, and will be studied by generations to come. All agreed that Richard Dimbleby's moving commentary was fully worthy of the grandeur of the occasion. Unknown to viewers and to most of his colleagues, Richard was suffering from cancer at the time. He had been living with it for the previous five years, during which he did not let it lose him a single day's work. However, in November 1965, when he had to enter St Thomas's Hospital for an operation, he asked his son David to make public why he was there, 'because he was strongly opposed to the idea of cancer being an unmentionable disease'.

The news of Dimbleby's illness, and the manner of its telling, gave his friends, known and unknown, sadness but increased their respect for him. Seven thousand wrote to him in hospital. They included several who suspected that they had cancer and now had been given the courage to consult their doctors. He also received letters from the King of Greece and the King of Jordan, books from Princess Alexandra and the Duke and Duchess of Kent, and four bottles of champagne from the Queen, delivered to the hospital by a guardsman. He died on 22 December

1965 at the age of 52, with Dilys his wife, and his sons David and Jonathan, who both were to follow him into broadcasting, at his bedside.

Westminster Abbey, which Dimbleby sometimes called his 'workshop', honoured him as no previous broadcaster had been honoured. On the morrow of his death the Dean suggested that a memorial service should be held in the great cathedral church where England salutes those who have rendered her outstanding service. Moreover, the Abbey decided that none of the substantial expense should fall upon either the Dimbleby family or the BBC.

The service on 4 January 1966 was a fitting farewell to the man who had so often been the spokesman of the BBC, and of the nation, at Westminster Abbey's great occasions. The Abbey was freshly adorned and floodlit in celebration of its 900 years. After every seat was taken, hundreds crowded into the cloister to watch the service on television. Five million viewers at home saw the memorial service, and six and a half million watched a recording at the end of the evening.

The BBC asked me to edit a book of tributes by his colleagues to recall some of the thousands of broadcasts he made and what it was like to work in broadcasting with him. We finished it in seven weeks, and over 200,000 copies were bought. The proceeds went to the Richard Dimbleby Cancer Fund established in his memory, which provided a research laboratory at St Thomas's. It was opened by the Queen three years after his death. In 1990 a memorial plaque, sculpted by his third son Nicholas, was installed in Poets' Corner in Westminster Abbey, the only such honour ever accorded to a broadcaster.

Richard Dimbleby's memory has also been kept green in other ways. One is the annual Dimbleby Lecture, established and televised by the BBC, which over two decades has brought important thought into the public domain. It was, for instance, in his Dimbleby Lecture that Roy Jenkins signalled the creation of the Social Democrats. In 1992 Lord Taylor, the new Lord Chief Justice, used the Dimbleby Lecture to draw attention to the social risks involved in inadequate funding of the system of justice. There is also the British Film and Television Academy's annual Richard Dimbleby Award for the most important contribution on screen in factual television.

Richard's lifelong friend and fellow war correspondent Wynford Vaughan-Thomas closed the Westminster Abbey Memorial Service commentary with these words:

'Ours is a transient art; our words and pictures make a powerful immediate impact, and then fade as if they had never been. But Richard brought a sense of permanence to our impermanent profession. We knew him as a simple man, a good man, and in the end a very brave man. He gave warmth to the spoken word, friendliness to the formal occasion, and dignity to the whole new world of broadcasting. We shall not easily forget him.'

7

Frank Gillard

'His skill as a manager equalled his flair as a reporter.'

Francis George Gillard, CBE 1961, OBE 1946, broadcaster, born Tiverton 1 December 1908, unmarried; BBC war correspondent North Africa, Italy, Normandy, Berlin 1940–45, Head of Radio and Television Programmes, Bristol 1945–55, Controller, West Region 1956–72, Director and later Managing Director, Radio 1963–70; Distinguished Fellow, Corporation for Public Broadcasting, USA 1960–66; Honorary LL.D. Exeter 1987.

While Richard Dimbleby was based in Cairo the British Forces had few victories for him to report. It fell to Frank Gillard, who was assigned to the Middle Eastern theatre in December 1942 as one of his successors, to chronicle the North African campaign of the Eighth Army under General Bernard Montgomery through to the day of final victory.

At that time Gillard was a 34-year-old bachelor who earlier that year had covered the ill-fated commando raid on Dieppe. He had joined the BBC in 1941 as a Talks Assistant and war correspondent (Southern Command) based in Bristol. He had grown up in Somerset, become a schoolmaster, and had frequently broadcast talks in the West Region.

Frank Gillard remained with the Eighth Army as it moved northwards across the Mediterranean, covering the landings in Sicily and Salerno. 'A tiger in chase of a story' was how a colleague described him. He got on well with both the troops and their commanders, and became a close friend of General Montgomery. As the Allies fought their way up Italy Gillard had singlehandedly to cover the activities of two armies.

W. J. Haley, shortly after he became the BBC's Editor-in-Chief in 1943, visited the Italian front to sort out a misunderstanding between Gillard and the Commander-in-Chief of the Allied Armies in Italy, General Harold Alexander, who had falsely accused him of breaking the war correspondents' rules (see Haley, p. 83). Haley had to spend ten days in Italy, which had a beneficial effect on Gillard's subsequent career. It was a stroke of luck for a relatively junior and unestablished recruit to the BBC staff to have the next Director-General to himself for ten days.

In 1944 Gillard became one of the chief members of the new *War Report* team which broadcast nightly on the progress of the liberating Allied Armies in north-west Europe. The Director of the War Reporting Unit was Howard Marshall, famous as a pre-war BBC sports commentator, who had swept into Paris with the victorious armies. By chance he discovered a transmitter said to be in touch with London, and broadcast from it a dispatch which he neglected to submit to censorship. This cost him his accreditation and he had to spend the rest of the war in London. His deputy suffered a nervous breakdown soon after D-Day.

The War Reporting Unit was therefore without an effective Director or Deputy Director. Gillard, as the senior man on the spot, took charge in Normandy. He quickly showed that his skill as a manager equalled his flair as a reporter. Montgomery insisted that Gillard should be present in his tent to witness the unconditional surrender of the German armies in Europe.

After the war Gillard returned to Bristol and shortly became Head of Programmes for the West Region, then an enormous area which stretched from Brighton to Land's End. It was one of the most sought-after places for BBC staff to work. It not only produced good programmes, showing one part of the region to another; it also contributed strongly to the national networks, both in radio and television, notably through its natural history programmes in both media, and through *Any Questions?* on what was still usually called the wireless.

Gillard supervised the West Region's programme output, but he also stayed close to the microphone, giving commentaries on major State occasions. In 1947 he accompanied the Royal Family on their tour of South Africa and was later the radio commentator at Princess Elizabeth's wedding. The next year at Buckingham Palace he described the silver wedding celebrations of King George VI and Queen Elizabeth, and he was one of three BBC correspondents travelling with Princess Elizabeth and the Duke of Edinburgh on their 1952 Commonwealth tour which ended abruptly in Kenya with the sudden news of the death of the King. Gillard was one of the radio commentators describing the Coronation procession the following year. In July 1955 he was moved to London as Chief Assistant to the Director of Sound Broadcasting.

In the spring of 1956, following Khrushchev's denunciation of Stalin, there was a thaw in what was then very much a Cold War. The Russians invited a small BBC delegation to inspect radio and television in Moscow,

Leningrad (now again St Petersburg) and Kiev. This was immediately accepted, and shortly after Easter Frank and I flew to the Soviet Union as the representatives respectively of radio and television programmes, along with the Director of External Broadcasting, who led the delegation, two senior engineers from radio and television, the Deputy Editor of News, and the Russian programme organiser from Bush House, who also acted as our private interpreter. Until then Moscow Radio and the BBC had had none of the international dealings that are normal between broadcasters.

We arrived just in time to watch the May Day parade in Red Square and to see how it was covered as an outside broadcast. We also watched a soccer match between the Moscow Dynamos and the Red Army, and visited countless studios and one factory in Leningrad which manufactured television sets. The day we flew down to Kiev Gillard remembered that, according to the Russian calendar, it was again Easter. To the slight discomfiture of our hosts he insisted that we Christians would all have to go to a service on Easter Day. His real reason was a desire to observe the impressive Midnight Liturgy for the Orthodox Easter in the Vladimir Cathedral at Kiev. The great church was crowded out, especially with young parents carrying infants on their shoulders, and very old women.

Our discussions with the Russians in that pre-*glasnost* time sought ways of opening up normal broadcasting relationships without the sacrifice of basic principles. They tended to founder when we brought up the question of the Soviet jamming of BBC programmes in Russian. But Gillard and I did return with one positive achievement. We got the names of two broadcasters who spoke excellent English and would be prepared to take part in radio hookup discussions of current affairs, subject to official permission. We also acquired their personal telephone numbers and soon found that the telephone could penetrate the Iron Curtain with unexpected ease.

That same year the Controller, West Region, Gerald Beadle, was promoted to become Director of Television in London and Frank Gillard returned to Bristol as his successor. It was one of the plum jobs in the BBC, and he did it very well. After seven happy years in Bristol Gillard returned to London in 1963 as Director of Sound Broadcasting.

Despite the highly successful *Radio Times*, the BBC seemed curiously reluctant to adopt the term 'radio' for general use. Some chauvinists thought it sounded rather American, unless qualified by the word 'sound'. But at that time Broadcasting House needed not only to modernise its vocabulary but also to adjust to living in the television age. The bright young men who had joined the BBC in the early 1920s were by then nearing retirement. The more adventurous of them had tended to move over into television. Those in senior positions who had chosen not to, or had not been accepted, were wont to complain that television was grabbing *their* audiences and *their* programme money. Morale in the senior branch of broadcasting was low.

Frank Gillard did not suffer from that kind of professional inferiority complex. He had been in charge of both media at Bristol, and handled them efficiently and harmoniously. He recognised that radio must change. The old programme departments in Broadcasting House had long required radical revision. He grasped these nettles courageously. The Features Department, once the flagship of broadcasting, had ceased to produce sustained programmes of quality and was living on its past reputation.

Gillard abolished it in 1964, not without an outcry. He also terminated *Children's Hour*, the familiar programme with which many of us had grown up, an action that resulted in a critical motion signed by sixty MPs. But *Children's Hour*'s daily listening audience had dropped to a mere 25,000 as children in their millions were watching the box.

Radio was changing both in technology and in programme style. VHF had come within reach of 98 per cent of the population, although only one home in three had acquired a VHF receiver. Transistors were becoming common. Carefully scripted talks were increasingly yielding to unscripted recorded discussions. *The World at One* started and so did the first correspondence column of the air, *Listening Post*, and *I'm Sorry I'll Read That Again*. *Woman's Hour* was once broadcast from Moscow, a by-product of our Russian visit.

Other changes involved the expansion of the daytime hours of the Third Network and the gradual introduction of the Music Programme. In 1967 Gillard started 'generic broadcasting'. Radio 1 filled the pop music gap left when an Act of Parliament effectively pulled the rug from under the new pirate radio stations by making advertising on them illegal. Radio 2 took over from the old Light Programme. Radio 3 incorporated the Third Programme, adding an early evening 'study session' and a sports service on Saturdays. The old Home Service became Radio 4.

Another of Gillard's innovations in 1967 was BBC local radio, with the start of experimental stations at Leicester, Sheffield and Merseyside. It was his dream to see them in every city, not as 'amplified juke boxes' but offering modern radio journalism geared to the interests of the local community.

Gillard retired from the BBC at the end of 1969. His skills were immediately sought by the newly formed Corporation for Public Broadcasting in the United States, which made him a Distinguished Fellow. Over several years he made a substantial contribution to the establishment of public service broadcasting in America. He also gave much useful counsel to the Australian Broadcasting Commission, as it was then named. The BBC continued to invite him to contribute broadcasts, both on radio and television, recalling various aspects of the Second World War.

Frank, who continued to look remarkably young, then turned his hand to a new enterprise. Realising that the generation which had pioneered broadcasting in Great Britain was rapidly fading away, he persuaded the BBC authorities to finance a large-scale oral history project. He and a few others of us interviewed those who had played a significant role in broadcasting's development, and encouraged them to record their experiences on to audiocassettes, as indiscreetly as they wished, with the assurance that the material would remain totally confidential until those directly concerned had died.

Later he organised a similar operation with film cameras to prepare material for some future television producer to use in AD 2022, the hundredth anniversary of the BBC's first broadcast from 2LO, assuming that the Corporation has not been driven out of existence by the bureaucratic complexities of Producer Choice, and that its passion for celebrating anniversaries has not waned.

8

Audrey Russell

'Elegantly dressed with a lovely speaking voice'

Muriel Audrey Russell, MVO 1976, born Dublin 29 June 1906 of Anglo-Irish parents; actress 1937; National Fire Service 1939–42; BBC reporter, war correspondent and Outside Broadcasts commentator 1942–51; freelance commentator on royal and State occasions 1951–84; lecturer on historical, artistic and royal matters; author of A Certain Voice *1984; fund raising and public relations committee of the Save the Children Fund 1973–77; died Woking, 9 August 1989, aged 83.*

Audrey Russell was the BBC's first woman news reporter, its only accredited female war correspondent during the Second World War, and an outstanding commentator on State occasions in the golden years of radio. For over a quarter of a century her calm authoritative voice brought pleasure to millions unable to watch ceremonial events on television.

Although Audrey Russell blazed the trail for reporters such as Sue McGregor and Kate Adie, the BBC employed women in important jobs even in its early days. From its very outset Reith had established the principle of equal pay for equal work regardless of sex, a practice not adopted everywhere in Britain to this day. Moreover,

71

women held some of the highest jobs. Hilda Matheson, who had been Lady Astor's secretary, became the first Head of a separate Talks Section in 1927. She developed the art of the scripted broadcast talk, not an essay or a lecture but the combination of ordered ideas with the projection of personality.

Under Hilda Matheson such people as H. G. Wells, Arnold Bennett, E. M. Forster, Harold Nicolson, Vernon Bartlett, Raymond Gram Swing and Stephen King-Hall were introduced to broadcasting. She left after a dispute with Charles Siepmann, her successor, which was essentially a clash of personalities. She continued, however, to be a staunch protagonist of the BBC in a number of books and articles.

Another was Mary Somerville, a New Zealander by birth, a Scot by upbringing and a graduate of the Oxford college whose name she bore. She was one of the pioneers of schools broadcasting and eventually became the first woman to achieve the exalted rank of Controller when she was placed in charge of the whole Talks division. Mary Somerville was a large woman, large in shape and large in heart. She opted for early retirement in 1955, at a time when many people who had chosen to stay in radio were dismayed that the balance of broadcasting was tipping in television's favour. Her departure was described as 'the ship leaving the sinking rats'.

My predecessor as Head of Television Talks, Mary Adams, had had a brilliant academic career as a scientist at Cambridge. She gave a series of talks on heredity in 1928 and was rapidly co-opted into the BBC's adult education department. She was one of only four producers at the very start of television and was responsible before the war for persuading such people as Kenneth Clark and John Betjeman to be televised.

Women radio producers abounded: Barbara Burnham in Drama, Marjorie Banks in Features, Janet Quigley in *Woman's Hour*, Jean Rowntree in Further Education, Anna Kallin and Leonie Cohn in Talks were only a few among many. In television Freda Lingstrom was the first Head of Children's Programmes. Doreen Stephens successfully ran the afternoon women's programmes and Monica Sims was one of Freda Lingstrom's successors in charge of programmes for children before she moved to Broadcasting House to become Controller of Radio 4 and Director of Radio Programmes. Other leading women in the television service were Grace Wyndham Goldie (pp. 135–44) and Joanna Spicer (pp. 171–6).

At Bush House Elisabeth Barker, daughter of Sir Ernst, the first Cambridge professor of political science, was an outstanding diplomatic correspondent and Sheila Grant Duff a brilliant Czech editor. Isa Benzie was the first Foreign Director and a key figure in the development of overseas broadcasting. Janet Adam Smith was an exceptionally talented first literary editor on *The Listener*. From the outset the BBC was well served by its female staff, but no one had breached the male bastion of news reporting until Audrey Russell did so in 1942. She was then 36.

Audrey Russell was born in Dublin and educated at a boarding school in Harrow and a finishing school in Paris. From her earliest days she was stagestruck. Tall, good-looking, elegantly dressed and with a lovely speaking voice, she had trained at the London School for Speech and Drama, and had become an actress before the Second World War. She had a small part in Laurence Housman's *Victoria Regina*, the first time the Lord Chamberlain permitted Queen Victoria to be portrayed on the stage, and also appeared in Clare Boothe Luce's play *The Women*.

Ten days after the outbreak of war she was called up for National Service as a firewoman. She fought fires during air-raids on London and when Dover was being shelled. It was when a BBC reporter did an interview with a tall elegant blonde in a steel helmet and dungarees that Audrey Russell's skill as a broadcaster was discovered. The Auxiliary Fire Service used her to make a number of successful broadcasts on its work. An especially successful one was her description of London's worst raid of the blitz on 10 May 1941, the night the House of Commons was bombed.

These vivid accounts of the devastation of the German attacks, and the behaviour of both suffering families and rescue services, led to an offer from the BBC's overseas service to join the team of the lively news and actuality magazine programme *Radio Newsreel*.

The Editor of *Radio Newsreel*, who had started it in 1940, was Peter Pooley, one of the ablest men who ever worked for the BBC. He sent Audrey to cover all sorts of home assignments, some of them very dangerous. She broadcast from army camps, ack-ack sites and barrage balloon stations, covering every kind of blitz and coastal raid. She successfully persuaded the reticent inventor of penicillin, Professor Alexander Fleming, to give her an important interview. Later the War Office accorded her full accreditation as a war correspondent to enter Europe with the *War Report* team.

At that time, before magnetic tape recorders were available in Britain, Audrey was supplied with what was called a 'portable' recording machine. It was a cumbersome instrument that weighed at least 35 pounds and cut acetate discs which Audrey carefully preserved at the right temperature by tucking them under her battle blouse. This had a curious effect on her elegant bust. She sent home many vivid dispatches from Belgium, Holland, Germany and Norway.

Audrey had long wanted to breach another male bastion: the Outside Broadcasts Department. Her chance came with the wedding of Princess Elizabeth and Prince Philip, the first of a long series of radio commentaries on royal and State occasions. Before television took over the major role in covering these ceremonies it was the task of the radio Outside Broadcasts commentator to act as the eye of the listener.

Audrey Russell was originally commissioned to provide descriptions of dresses and other details giving the 'women's angle'. She did this well, but she also provided, in well-constructed and beautifully modulated sentences, word pictures which enabled those listening, both at home and at the far ends of the earth, to visualise the colourful scene. She covered the Queen's Coronation, the funerals of King George VI and Sir Winston Churchill, the weddings of Princesses Margaret and Alexandra, and (for the Canadian Broadcasting Corporation) of the Prince of Wales. She also went on many Royal Tours abroad. Though constantly reporting on royalty she never took on the awe-struck tones some speakers used, and despite often feeling nervous, she always managed to appear unflappable. Her research work in preparation for these broadcasts was meticulous.

Among the honours Audrey accumulated were the Gold Medal of the Poetry Society in 1934, the Freedom of the City of London in 1967 and the MVO in 1976 from the Queen, who also gave her a hand-embroidered chair – her proudest possession. She never married, though before the war she had become the fiancée of the heir to a baronetcy. His remark, 'It seems you only come to life when talking about the stage', signalled the beginning of the end of their engagement.

9

William Haley

'I am going to Fleet Street.'

William John Haley, KCMG 1946, born 24 May 1901, married 1921 Edith Susie Gibbons, two sons two daughters; reporter, Manchester Evening News *1922, managing editor 1930, director, Manchester Guardian and Evening News Ltd; director, Press Association and Reuters 1939–43; Editor-in-Chief, BBC 1943, Director-General 1944–52; editor,* The Times *1952–66; editor-in-chief,* Encyclopædia Britannica *1968–69; President, National Book League 1955–62; Honorary Fellow, Jesus College, Cambridge; honorary degrees from Cambridge and Dartmouth, New Hampshire; died 6 September 1987, aged 86.*

W. J. Haley's important role at the BBC came about through a complicated series of events, in many ways typical of the Corporation's development. When Reith left in 1938 there was no shortage of candidates to succeed him. His own preference was for Cecil Graves, a man of great charm who at that time was Programme Controller. He had earlier been the first Head of the Empire Service. But Graves was a Roman Catholic by conversion, and in those pre-war days the likelihood of the Board appointing a Catholic to be Director-General of the BBC was negligible. One of the best-known Governors, H. A. L. Fisher, a former president of the Board of Education and Warden of New College, encapsulated the views of the Establishment in a letter to the BBC Chairman: 'I think it would be quite impossible that the supreme executive control of one of the most important organs of public education in this country should be placed in Roman Catholic hands.'

The newspapers canvassed the names of several distinguished men from outside the BBC. One was Sir Hector Hetherington who had just become the Principal of Glasgow University after nine years as Vice-Chancellor of the University of Liverpool. Hetherington lobbied the Governors, arguing that what this important organ of public education needed, in succession to Reith, was a professional educationist, not from Oxbridge. And who, by inference, was more suitable than one who had headed two provincial universities?

The Governors accepted Hetherington's thesis but not Hetherington himself. They offered the post to a different academic principal, F. W. Ogilvie, the Vice-Chancellor of Queen's University, Belfast. Frederick Ogilvie was a man of great intellectual capacity and personal charm. The one quality he lacked was ability to manage a large organisation.

Within a year Britain was at war, and the BBC became answerable to the Ministry of Information. Ogilvie allowed the BBC's wartime finances and administration to degenerate into a serious state. In October 1941 Brendan Bracken, the Minister of Information, who was much worried by the situation in the BBC, persuaded the General Manager of the Gas, Light and Coke Company, Robert W. Foot, to spend three months in Broadcasting House looking into the books and writing a report on the way the Corporation was being managed. On his first day there the phone rang and a voice with a Scottish burr said, 'Mr Foot? Reith here. You will be wondering what your tasks are. Your first task is to get rid of Ogilvie. Your second task is to get rid of yourself. Goodbye.'

Foot completed his examination and produced a severely critical report. It convinced the Governors that it was time for Ogilvie to leave. They had been greatly impressed by Foot's administrative ability and financial acumen, and believed he might make a good successor. But he had no experience of broadcasting. In the more ecumenical days of wartime Roman Catholicism was no longer considered an automatic bar, so they opted for a diarchy. Sir Cecil Graves, the Deputy Director-General, as he had in the meantime become, would be responsible for the output, and Robert Foot for the administration.

Forcing a Director-General to resign seems to be an action that BBC Governors take secretively over lunch. Harold Nicolson, then recently appointed to the Board, recorded in his diary on 26 January 1942:

To Grosvenor House where we have a hush meeting of the BBC Board. We decide to retire Ogilvie and put Graves and Foot as Joint Directors-General in his place. I am sure that this is right, as Ogilvie is too noble a character for rough war-work. Yet I mind deeply in a way. This clever, high-minded man being pushed aside. I hate it. But I agree.

The BBC staff greeted the idea of a diarchy somewhat frivolously. Some said the purpose of appointing two DGs was to have one to say 'Yes' to the Ministry of Information and the other to say 'No' to the staff. To others they were collectively known as One Foot In The Graves. In fact the diarchy worked harmoniously, but only for a year, for in June 1943 failing health forced Graves to retire.

Foot urgently needed a programme man at his side to

replace Graves. Bracken had an unexpected suggestion, backed by Churchill: Edward R. Murrow, the great American war correspondent whose broadcasts to the United States had generated so much support for Britain in the darkest days. Murrow thought about it carefully, discussed it with Roosevelt's friend Justice Felix Frankfurter, and finally asked not to be considered.

News was the most important programme ingredient in wartime. The Governors urged Foot to look to Fleet Street to provide an Editor-in-Chief. Reuters suggested one of their directors, William John Haley. He had been editor and managing director of the *Manchester Evening News*, the money-making partner of the *Manchester Guardian*, of which he had also been a young managing director. Haley had left school at 15 and become a telegraphist on *The Times*. He was remarkably well read. The Governors appointed him Editor-in-Chief in September 1943. He was then 42.

One of Haley's first assignments was to visit the battle-front in Italy to settle a rather petty row that had developed between the Commander-in-Chief, General Harold Alexander, and Frank Gillard, the chief BBC war correspondent in the Italian theatre. Alexander had accused Gillard of operating a secret transmitter, thereby 'beating the gun', as he put it, on the release of military news, and would not accept Gillard's indignant denial. Gillard suggested that someone impartial should arbitrate. He wanted this nonsense cleared up emphatically, because lurking behind it was a general challenge to swift and candid war reporting. The campaign was not going well, and there were Generals who considered that the less said about it the better. Alexander said he had already asked Brendan Bracken, the Minister of Information, to come out to adjudicate the matter. In the event Haley, who had only been in the BBC for a few days, was asked to take off for Italy, in place of Bracken.

Haley had been suffering from pernicious anaemia and the long air journey, in an uncomfortable military aircraft which had to take a route out over the Atlantic and across Africa rather than along the Mediterranean, was a considerable strain. However, he and Gillard were quickly able to convince Alexander that the fact that he could hear news of developments on the Italian battle front from the BBC before they had been reported to him by his own units might have something to do with his own interior lines of communication. Gillard also had chapter and verse to demolish other petty allegations of inaccuracy. Haley defended Gillard magnificently throughout. The Generals around the C-in-C were totally silenced, and Alexander withdrew the charges most graciously. Cordial relations were re-established and the matter was never mentioned to Gillard again.

So the primary purpose of Haley's visit to Italy was accomplished within a few hours of his arrival. As there was no prospect of an early return flight to London, Alexander suggested that Gillard should take Haley on a general tour of the army fronts. This involved an arduous ten-day tour of several hundred miles, during which Gillard introduced Haley to division and corps commanders and finally to General Mark Clark, the American Commander-in-Chief of the Fifth Army, and to General Bernard Montgomery of the Eighth Army.

During the long hours when they were alone together Gillard ventured to tell the new Editor-in-Chief that he thought the BBC's provision for British forces overseas was inadequate. What they received by shortwave from the BBC was the General Overseas Service, which made them feel like expatriates. What they wanted to hear was the Home Service or the Forces Programme, so that they could feel linked with families at home who were listening to the same material. Whenever Haley and Gillard had a chance to talk briefly with troops in twos or threes behind the lines they invariably made the same point.

Haley returned to London on Christmas Eve 1943, well laden with oranges, nuts and other delicacies no longer obtainable in England, and with his first new programme recommendation formulated. The Board accepted early in the New Year his proposal that the Forces Programme in the United Kingdom should merge with a totally reconstituted General Overseas Service to form the General Forces Programme, broadcast at home and on shortwave to servicemen in all theatres of war. The General Forces Programme, which after the war became the Light Programme, began on 27 February 1944.

The very next month, to general surprise, Robert Foot resigned the Director-Generalship to become chairman of the Mining Association of Great Britain, a lobby dedicated to preventing the nationalisation of the coal pits. It was a curiously shortsighted decision which left the BBC needing its fourth Director-General in only two years. The Governors were weary of these constant changes at the top. William Haley had only been in the BBC for seven months but they had no hesitation in selecting him for the succession.

As a professional journalist Haley took a great interest in the development of BBC news. Scarcely a month after D-Day he recommended to the Governors a scheme to establish a post-war corps of BBC foreign correspondents. Before the war the newspaper interests had successfully prevented the BBC from gathering its own news abroad. The experience of *War Report*, Haley argued, showed it was the BBC's duty to supplement the news it received from the agencies by dispatches from its own men – they were only men in those sexist days. The scheme was approved and, equally important, the Treasury sanctioned the substantial expenditure of foreign currency involved.

Between 1942 and 1944 I had been seconded from the BBC German Service to the Political Warfare Executive to join its mission in the United States, to liaise with the Voice of America on broadcasting to Europe. With this recent experience of the United States I was chosen to be the first regular correspondent in Washington. Haley briefed me before I went, stressing that I must not only report events but also explain them in the American context, and at the same time refrain from making any comment myself on what was going on.

He also told me that he was at that time under strong pressure from the new Labour Prime Minister, Clement Attlee, to broadcast an appeal to the 40,000-odd dockers, then on unofficial strike for higher wages at many of Britain's ports, to return to work. Their action was causing the country great hardship. Haley said he had just told the Prime Minister the appeal could indeed be made. But he would also have to allow a reply from the dockers. Attlee withdrew his request.

Sir William Haley (he was knighted in 1946) was not only concerned with the BBC's adjustment to peacetime conditions and the re-establishment of its independence from government interference. He was also busy planning the development of radio. He inaugurated the Third Programme in September 1944, offering a cultural cornucopia of plays, operas and intellectual talks, subsequently published in *The Listener*. Critics, of whom there were several, sometimes called these talks 'the printed word in spoke'. But the Third Programme also commanded loyal, if not large-scale, support, and it was emulated in Italy.

Haley was at first less interested in the emergent television service which restarted, after being closed down during the war, just in time to cover the 1946 Victory Parade. But television gradually established itself and expanded. More studio space was needed and in 1949 the BBC acquired thirteen acres on the White City site of the Franco-British Exhibition of 1908 on which to build its new Television Centre. Pending the completion of Television Centre, it also bought from the J. Arthur Rank Organisation as 'temporary accommodation' Britain's first purpose-built film studio at nearby Lime Grove, a small street near Shepherd's Bush Green.

The Lime Grove studio had been created in 1914 for the Gaumont-British Picture Corporation and over the years had produced many famous films, such as *Evergreen* and other successful musicals starring Jessie Matthews, the Jack Hulbert and Arthur Askey comedies, *Fanny by Gaslight*, *The Wicked Lady*, *The Man in Grey* and many more. During the war it had been the base for the Gaumont-British newsreel. The Lime Grove studio space was rapidly converted to television use and Studio D was ready for the production of *Children's Hour* by May 1950. The planning and development of the White City site continued under Sir William Haley but in April 1951 there was a major hold-up owing to government limitations on capital expenditure, caused by the costs of the Korean war.

Meanwhile the Governors decided in 1950 that television deserved a seat on the Board of Management, which had been established by Haley three years earlier. The man chosen to be the first Director of Television was not its current Controller, Norman Collins, but George Barnes, holder of the egregious title of Director of the

Spoken Word. Collins, a successful novelist (*London Belongs to Me*) and an ardent protagonist of television, abruptly resigned, invested his pension entitlement in one of the new companies hoping for a commercial television franchise, and became a leading lobbyist for a system that would break the BBC's monopoly.

Haley had previously steered the BBC through one of its regular inquisitions prior to the renewal of its Charter, the Committee of Inquiry chaired by Lord Beveridge, the Liberal whose wartime report on social security was the foundation of the welfare state. Beveridge was a cantankerous chairman, who managed to introduce into the Committee's report his petulant personal resentment at not having been invited to participate in a radio programme celebrating the Wordsworth Centenary. The bulky Beveridge Report included one hundred recommendations. By and large they supported Haley's own proposals, though usually with some kind of criticism.

More important in the long run was a minority report. This was written by Selwyn Lloyd, then a 44-year-old Conservative MP, advocating the establishment of a commercial television service. By the time Parliament got around to dealing with the future of television a powerful commercial lobby had persuaded the new Conservative government to espouse Selwyn Lloyd's views. This was not at all to Haley's liking, and he gladly accepted an offer to become the editor of *The Times*, the paper on which he had started his journalistic career as a telegraphist.

Sir William had by then been Director-General for eight years but he was still a remote figure for many of the staff. Nevertheless he felt he ought to visit every office in Broadcasting House to say goodbye personally. He tried the room of one producer who was out. The secretary had no idea who the visitor was. After waiting a long time for the producer to return Haley said, 'I'm afraid I must be going now.' 'Where are you going to?' she asked. 'I am going to Fleet Street,' he said. 'Well, you can get a number fifteen bus the other side of Oxford Circus,' she told him helpfully.

Although Haley was painfully shy, he was, in my view, a good Director-General. He established the post-war pattern of BBC broadcasting. He modernised the management structure. He fought hard to keep the BBC securely independent of government interference. He supported the staff when they were attacked, and he adumbrated the ideals of public broadcasting eloquently and persuasively.

10

Ian Jacob

*'If the BBC is found for the first time
to be suppressing significant items of
news its reputation would rapidly
vanish.'*

*Edward Ian Claud Jacob, Lt-Gen, GBE 1960, KBE 1946, CB
1944, DL, born 27 September 1899, married 1924 Cecil
Treherne (died 1991, two sons); Military Assistant Secretary,
Committee of Imperial Defence 1938, Military Assistant Secretary to the War Cabinet 1939–46; Controller, BBC European
Services 1946, Director, Overseas Services 1947–52, Director-
General 1952–60; president, European Broadcasting Union
1950–60; Assistant Military Secretary to the War Cabinet
1952; chairman, Covent Garden Market Authority 1961–66;
US Legion of Merit; died Woodbridge, Suffolk, 24 April 1993,
aged 93.*

I first met General Sir Ian Jacob in the United States in
July 1948 at the National Convention of the Democratic
Party in Philadelphia. That was the one which renomi-
nated Harry Truman for the presidency. The left wing of
the Democratic Party under Henry Wallace, the right-
wing Dixiecrats from the South, several trade union
leaders who preferred General Eisenhower, and one of
the sons of President Franklin Roosevelt had all wanted

to dump Truman. Nevertheless he won and, against the odds, was to win the presidential election later that year.

I was then the BBC's Washington correspondent. Sir Ian was Director of the Overseas Services. During the war, as Military Assistant Secretary to the War Cabinet, he had accompanied Churchill to all his meetings with Roosevelt. Jacob had had close dealings with many of the American political and military leaders, whom he depicted with candid perception in the private diary he kept, quoted at length in the biography written in 1991 by Sir Charles Richardson, *From Churchill's Secret Circle to the BBC*. Jacob had also travelled with Prime Minister Clement Attlee to North America in November 1945 for discussions with the Americans and the Canadians on atomic weapons.

Sir Ian was keen to see what an American political convention was like, and he had been particularly interested in the attempt of some misguided wellwishers to draft General Eisenhower to replace President Truman. Eisenhower had told the Democrats, just before the convention opened, 'I will not, at this time, identify myself with any political party.' Four years later he was to be the winning Republican candidate.

We sat together in the sweltering heat in Philadelphia. It was the first time an American National Convention had been held under television lights, and the last year that it met in a hall without airconditioning. The temperature inside was 110 degrees Fahrenheit. I introduced him to two BBC contributors he was anxious to meet, Raymond Gram Swing and Alistair Cooke, and I tried to answer as best I could the penetrating questions he posed about the American procedure.

Sir Ian was a trim, athletic man of medium height with great charm of manner. He had a very quick mind, as befitted someone who had passed first into the Staff

College with record high marks and had also shone at the Royal Military Academy, Woolwich, and at King's College, Cambridge. He was a child of the Raj, the son of Field-Marshal Sir Claud Jacob who had been Chief of the General Staff in Simla, and he was the last of twenty-nine male members of the Jacob family to have served as a professional soldier in India.

But Sir Ian was not a typical brass hat. During the war his contribution, and it had been a great one, had been as a government official rather than as a fighting soldier. He had been the principal controller of military information for the War Cabinet, and one of the three men who made sure that its decisions were co-ordinated smoothly. Wherever Churchill went, and he made thirteen wartime journeys abroad, Jacob would set up an efficiently run temporary office through which outgoing orders and incoming reports flowed without pause.

Churchill had a very high regard for Jacob, and secured his gradual promotion from Colonel to Major-General. But Jacob had not been in command of troops in the field, and he knew that in peacetime he could look for no further promotion as a professional soldier.

By the end of the war the European Service at Bush House had achieved a very high reputation. It had slowly grown into the largest and the most trusted foreign-language radio service in the world. Yet by the end of 1945 it was in grave danger of disintegrating. Many of the talented wartime broadcasters it had attracted were returning to their pre-war pursuits as journalists, dons, actors or European statesmen. Others had been recruited into the new United Nations radio department. Some, like me, had been posted abroad to form the BBC's first corps of foreign correspondents. Few were keen to make a peacetime career in foreign-language broadcasting. And the service needed a new controller. Ivone Kirkpatrick, who had been seconded from the Foreign Office, had been transferred to the Control Commission for Germany.

It was Kirkpatrick who suggested to Sir William Haley, the Director-General, that Jacob might be the ideal man to arrest the seepage from Bush House and revive its morale. His experience at the nerve centre of the war had given him an invaluable knowledge of world affairs. For six years he had been privy to every secret of State. Haley had met Jacob in the spring of 1944 when broadcasting preparations for D-Day were being made, and had been greatly impressed by his brisk and intelligent way of tackling problems. He also recognised that Jacob carried substantial weight in Whitehall and would be able to fend off some of the threatened cuts in the grant-in-aid that financed the BBC's broadcasts to foreign countries.

With the approval of the Governors, Sir Ian – his wartime service had been recognised by a knighthood in the Birthday Honours List of 1946 – was shortly afterwards appointed Controller of the European Service. At Bush House he was an outstanding success.

The following year Haley reorganised the structure of the BBC, creating the Board of Management with five members. It was a logical move to combine the two divisions which broadcast abroad, European and Overseas, and Jacob was promoted to take charge of all external broadcasting with the title of Director of Overseas Service. In that capacity in February 1950 he chaired an international conference at Torquay which set up the European Broadcasting Union. Jacob was elected its first president and he retained that office until he retired from broadcasting ten years later.

When Churchill again became Prime Minister, in October 1951, he took the Defence portfolio for himself as well. 'Jacob, you must come back,' he said immediately, and persuaded Haley to second Sir Ian back to the Ministry of Defence to become his Chief Staff Officer, before setting off on a visit to Washington and Ottawa.

It did not take Churchill long to discover that being Minister of Defence in peacetime was much less interesting than during a world war. When he returned from North America he announced that Earl Alexander of Tunis would take over the Ministry of Defence as soon as he completed his term as Governor-General of Canada. Jacob was less than elated. He thought soldiers made bad ministers. With some reluctance he started his temporary job as Chief Staff Officer to the Minister of Defence and Deputy Secretary to the Cabinet in May 1952. The next month he received a letter from Haley announcing his decision to leave the BBC and become editor of *The Times*.

At a routine meeting the following day Churchill said, 'I see that your Director-General is going. Who will get the job?' Jacob replied, 'I don't know, but I suppose I have some claims to it.' He had indeed. Though he had not been concerned with domestic broadcasting he was greatly respected by the other members of the Board of Management. Moreover, he had made no enemies. Gerald Beadle, who at that time was the Controller, West Region, later told me that he and all the other Regional Controllers (a formidable collection of robber barons) had previously informed Lord Simon of Wythenshawe, who was nearing the end of his term as BBC Chairman, that they would resign *en masse* if George Barnes, the Director of Television, were appointed DG.

The outgoing Governors recommended the appointment of Jacob, but as he was still at the Ministry of Defence the senior member of the Board of Management, Sir Basil Nicolls, was made Acting Director-General. He was then the Director of Home Broadcasting and within a year of the retiring age. Lord Simon's successor as Chairman, Sir Alexander Cadogan OM, recently the head of the Foreign Office, accompanied by the new Vice-Chairman, Marshal of the RAF Lord Tedder, formally offered the job to Sir Ian in October, diffidently asking whether they might avoid referring to his military rank. Some press comment complained that the combination of a senior civil servant, a Marshal of the RAF and a Major-General at the top of the BBC was 'too many brass hats'.

Jacob was released from the Ministry of Defence to become Director-General on 1 December 1952. He got on well with Cadogan, with whom he had worked during the war. Indeed he had a happy relationship with most of the Governors throughout his tenure. The only one with whom he had difficulties was Lady Rhys Williams. She was highly intelligent and most industrious, but did not appreciate the difference between policy making and executive action. She was neither the first nor the last member of the Board to muddle those roles.

Helped by the outstandingly successful coverage of the Coronation, by 1957 television had become the dominant broadcasting medium. The extra income engendered by the growth in television licences made this period relatively free from financial worries. Haley's Director-Generalship had been a time of austerity, matching that of the country. He had insisted on approving personally, for example, a proposal to provide a new set of tyres for an Outside Broadcasts van. Jacob surprised the Board of Management early in his reign by declaring that anyone who thought the BBC was poor should get that out of his head immediately. The BBC was a rich organisation and he did not want to hear any more depressing talk about poverty and parsimony.

He took a great interest in the development of current affairs, especially in television, for which I became responsible in 1954. He was insistent on accuracy and impartiality. He vigorously replied to one noble complainant's charge of bias:

'I can assure you that the question of impartiality, which is one of the key points in the conduct of broadcasting, is bound to be the continual concern of whoever is in charge, and has certainly been mine. You say there is a large body of opinion that is convinced that the BBC is red. That remark does not surprise me in the least because there is an equally large body of opinion which is convinced that the BBC is a hide-bound institution, 'the prop of the Establishment', and rootedly opposed to anything left-wing. This is bound to be the situation of anybody who tries to steer a course down the centre.'

Jacob was also assiduous in working to remove constraints on the BBC's liberty of action. A particularly irksome restriction on the handling of political news was the so-called 'Fourteen-Day Rule'. This had originally been established by the Governors during the war to protect the BBC from what they regarded as an abuse of power by the coalition government, when Rab Butler broadcast a talk lobbying for his 1944 Education Act which was about to be discussed in the House of Commons. The rule was intended to prevent parliamentary debates due to take place within the next fourteen days from being prejudiced.

However, it had become a rod for the BBC's back because it often blocked current affairs programmes from discussing the most important topical issue, forcing them on to minor matters instead. Moreover, no one outside the BBC was aware of this constraint. In 1953 and 1954 Jacob tried hard, in meetings with the political parties, to have the rule rescinded but Churchill and Attlee were adamant that it must be kept.

In February 1955 I encouraged the chairman of *In the News*, a regular television discussion programme among four MPs, to protest publicly against not being allowed to discuss the testing of the hydrogen bomb because a House of Commons defence debate was scheduled within the coming fortnight. This brought the existence of the rule out into the open.

Jacob enlisted the support of the leaders of the Independent Television Authority against the Fourteen-Day Rule and encouraged us to draw the attention of audiences to occasions when it prevented an important topical broadcast. In the press it was openly derided. Jacob told the government in July 1955 that the BBC would no longer regard the rule as binding unless what had been a matter of convention was prescribed under the Postmaster-General's reserve powers. This was done by Dr Charles Hill, the PMG, with the support of Churchill and Attlee. It took a year and a half of pressure, both by reasoned argument and by public ridicule, before Harold Macmillan suspended the rule indefinitely.

One day Churchill telephoned Jacob to say that he had heard from the Governor of Cyprus that *Panorama* had filmed an interview with Archbishop Makarios – Churchill pronounced his name to rhyme with Zacharias. The Prime Minister said the Archbishop was an enemy of Britain and the interview ought not to be shown.

Jacob promised to review the film personally and brought his Chief Assistant, Harman Grisewood, to look at it with me in one of the Lime Grove viewing theatres. In reply to one of the sharper questions put to him by Woodrow Wyatt, Makarios gave a shifty look sideways before making a bland reply. Jacob said to me afterwards,

'You know, television gives current affairs a further dimension of truth. If I had heard that reply on radio, or read it in the paper, I'd have taken it at its face value. But having seen that shifty look I knew you could not trust him an inch. I'll tell the PM we'll transmit the interview.' Churchill's response was 'Jacob, I would never have expected this of you.'

There was an interesting sequel. In 1956 Makarios was deported as a terrorist to cool his heels in the Seychelles. Following the pattern of British imperial history he returned, in the course of time, as the first President of Cyprus. This time *Panorama* sent Chris Chataway to film an interview with him on his way back through Athens. The camera was set up in the city's main square. Chris asked a pointed question about Makarios's promise to co-operate with the Turkish minority on Cyprus. Again the Archbishop gave a shifty look downwards before making a similarly bland reply. In fact a little dog in the square had just started to pee against Makarios's leg. Where was Jacob's further dimension of television truth that time?

Early in his reign Sir Ian had to decide the BBC's stance *vis-à-vis* the new commercial television. At first it was one of peaceful coexistence, with discussions about sharing the Crystal Palace transmitting mast or covering royal occasions where there was only room for one camera. Gradually the relationship changed as ITV took over an increasing share of the television audience. At the end of 1957 the ratio dropped as low as 28:72. Jacob was adamant that a good case for a second BBC channel should be made to the next broadcasting committee of inquiry and asked my department to make a special documentary film which would show how the BBC worked. Richard Cawston produced *This is the BBC*, which won several awards and was viewed with great interest by the

Pilkington Committee after Jacob's retirement.

The most serious threat to the BBC's independence came during the Suez crisis, when the Eden government wished to prevent the Overseas Service from reporting, in its regular press reviews, editorials critical of the bombardment of Egypt. Jacob's reaction was forthright. 'If the BBC is found for the first time to be suppressing significant items of news its reputation would rapidly vanish, and the harm to the national interest done in that event would enormously outweigh any damage caused by displaying to the world the workings of a free democracy,' he declared.

The government decided to cut the Bush House grant-in-aid by a million pounds as a punitive gesture. Jacob and Cadogan called on Rab Butler and managed to reduce the threatened cut by half before the Director-General flew off to a Commonwealth broadcasting conference in Australia. During his absence his stance was stoutly maintained by his deputies, and after Eden's resignation that challenge to the BBC's editorial independence was lifted.

In 1924 Ian Jacob had married Cecil, the daughter of another distinguished officer, Surgeon Major-General Sir Francis Treherne. After his death his Georgian house at Woodbridge, Suffolk, became the Jacob family home. Lady Jacob had great charm. It was a very happy marriage which lasted for sixty-six years. Sir Ian retired at the end of 1959, shortly after his sixtieth birthday, and the next day was awarded the GBE.

However, his retirement was by no means the end of his long public service. In 1963 he was the principal author of the seminal Ismay–Jacob report on the central organisation of defence. This was the blueprint which led to substantial unification changes in the defence establishment, commissioned by Harold Macmillan and Peter Thorneycroft, and implemented by Earl Mountbatten. Jacob himself regarded his role in the defence reorganisation as the most important single act in a life ninety-three years long. History may prefer to regard him as the Director-General who brought the BBC into the television age. He was, in my view, a much underrated DG. He was overshadowed, metaphorically as well as physically, by those two giants Lord Reith and Sir Hugh Greene. Yet he successfully piloted the BBC through more turbulent waters than Reith or Greene ever encountered.

11

Hugh Greene

*'I was like a Beefeater tampering with
the Crown Jewels.'*

*Hugh Carleton Greene, KCMG 1964, OBE 1959, born 15
November 1910, married 1st 1934 Helga Guinness, two sons,
2nd 1951 Elaine Shaplen two sons, 3rd 1970 Tatjana Sais (died
1981), 4th 1984 Sarah Grahame; journalist,* Daily Telegraph,
*Berlin 1934, Warsaw 1939; BBC German News Editor 1940
after service with the RAF; Controller of Broadcasting in
British Zone of Germany 1946–48; Head of BBC East European
Service 1949–50; Head of Emergency Information Service,
Malaya 1950–51; Assistant Controller, BBC Overseas Services
1952–55, Controller, Overseas Services 1955–56; Chairman,
Federal Commission of Inquiry into Broadcasting, Rhodesia
and Nyasaland 1955; Director of Administration, BBC 1956–
58, Director, News and Current Affairs 1958–59, Director-
General 1960–69, Governor, BBC 1969–71; vice-president,
European Broadcasting Union 1963–69; chairman,* The Bodley
Head *1969; chairman, European-Atlantic Action Committee
on Greece; trustee,* The Observer *1969–76; honorary degrees
East Anglia 1969, Open University 1973; died 19 February
1987, aged 76.*

Hugh Carleton Greene joined the BBC in October 1940,
as the News Editor and Head of the German Section,

where I was the News Talks Editor. A very tall, thin, bespectacled, shambling man, he had just been released from interrogating German pilots shot down by the RAF. The authorities felt that his abilities would be more valuably used in improving the BBC's news programmes broadcast to Germany. His arrival at Broadcasting House immediately boosted the morale and the status of our somewhat amateur and overworked part of the new European Service.

He came to lead the German Section, at the age of 29, already with a substantial reputation. He had been one of the best-known journalists in Berlin, a chief correspondent of the *Daily Telegraph*, before being kicked out, with five other newsmen, as a reprisal for the expulsion of a Nazi propagandist from Britain. His experience of the Nazi regime, at the height of its malign power, was an important factor in shaping his own libertarian political stance. He had also reported the outbreak of the war from Poland, and covered its early stages from many other countries.

Moreover, Hugh came from a remarkable family. Three of the four sons of Charles Greene, the headmaster of Berkhamsted School, were included in *Who's Who* before they were 30: Raymond, the distinguished physician and Everest mountaineer, Graham the novelist, and Hugh, who had become an outstanding journalist after coming down from Oxford. Hugh used his middle name Carleton in his journalistic by-line to distinguish himself, as he said, from all the other Hugh Greenes in the business. He dropped it, as no longer necessary, when he was knighted in 1964.

The eldest of the four brothers, Herbert Greene, was a poet who led a march on Broadcasting House in protest against his younger brother's decision as Director-General to move the main evening radio news bulletin from its hallowed time of 9 o'clock to 10 o'clock. Hugh himself admitted: 'I was like a Beefeater tampering with the Crown Jewels.' I told him his watchword should be: 'Am I my brother's timekeeper?'

Hugh Greene's contribution to the BBC German broadcasts was immense. He flew in a Mosquito over German-occupied Norway to neutral Stockholm to study how the BBC output sounded through the barrage of Nazi jamming. As a result he totally changed the style in which the German news was written and delivered. It became a thoroughly professional operation and contributed strongly to the European Service's reputation. He also became a well-known broadcaster himself, both as a news commentator and in a kind of *Brains Trust* weekly discussion with R. H. S. Crossman, Lindley Fraser and Marius Goring – I was the producer.

In 1941 Greene helped to create a sort of peaceful coexistence between the BBC's German Section and its political masters, the Political Warfare Executive (PWE), operating from their hush-hush country headquarters in the stable block of Woburn Abbey, the home of the Duke of Bedford. Each faction had been deeply suspicious of the other. PWE prepared a weekly directive, instructing the BBC German Section what line to take. They also approved the talks we intended to broadcast. Very often the situation changed so much that the PWE instructions ceased to be valid. Some in what was known as 'the Country' thought the BBC German Section must be staffed with saboteurs. From Broadcasting House the PWE directives often seemed wildly irrelevant.

Dick Crossman was made Head of the German Department of PWE in 1940. He was also regularly broadcasting talks in German for the BBC, so he had a foot in each camp. He suggested that Greene and I should drive down to Woburn every Friday night and hammer out a German policy directive for the coming week which would make sense to both sides.

We enjoyed this weekly relief from the strain of the blitz, and Greene always maintained that the beer available at Woburn helped to lubricate what was still sometimes an abrasive relationship. He had a connoisseur's interest in beer and was eventually to become a director of the family brewery, Greene King and Sons Ltd, founded by his great-grandfather.

The final rapprochement between PWE and the BBC German Section was clinched in the summer of 1941 at a cricket match, when a Bush House team, captained by Greene, the wicket-keeper, challenged a PWE eleven. A return match was played the following year. During the game a messenger panted on to the field to tell us of the fall of Tobruk and the humiliating surrender of its South African garrison. We reminded ourselves of Plymouth Hoe and played on. Half a century later 'The Bushmen' still thrives as a cricket and dining club.

After the war Greene was seconded to the British Control Commission to reorganise German broadcasting. He is remembered with affection in Germany for his work there, and for the spirit of independence he imbued in his staff. But in later years he had to admit that he had failed to prevent the selection of senior broadcasting staff on a strictly proportionate political basis.

The next period of Hugh Greene's career involved a return to political warfare, first as Head of the East European Service at Bush House during the early days of the cold war, and then as a propagandist with the British Army in Malaya at the time of the attempted Communist takeover.

Sir Ian Jacob, the BBC Director-General in the 1950s,

began to groom Hugh Greene as his successor. He was made Director of Administration, and then Director of News and Current Affairs. Greene frequently said that his first task in that latter role was to restore freedom to the News Division, which under its then editor, the late Tahu Hole, had become known as the Kremlin of the BBC (see Hole, pp. 123–33). Indeed he often boasted that his greatest achievement in broadcasting was to get rid of the oppressive Hole. He did this shortly after he moved into Reith's old office in January 1960 as 'the other great DG', to quote John Freeman.

The other immediate tasks facing Greene were to reclaim from ITV a decent share of the television audience, and to present a good BBC case to the Committee on Broadcasting headed by Sir Harry Pilkington. This had been established to assess the achievements of the rival television networks and to make recommendations on the allocation of further channels.

After Pilkington had reported, perhaps embarrassingly warmly, in the BBC's favour, Greene came to Television Centre for his quarterly meeting with the senior staff. We greeted his arrival with a storm of applause, to which he responded with the words: 'You're behaving like Russians, clapping yourselves.'

The Pilkington Report led to the creation of BBC2, which involved changing the traditional British television transmission standards from 405 to 625 lines, in the Ultra High Frequency band instead of in a Very High Frequency band. This was a major technical undertaking. It also involved a greater commitment to educational broadcasting on television. In 1971 Lord Goodman, on behalf of the Harold Wilson Cabinet, conducted detailed discussions with Sir Hugh on the establishment of the Open University, to ascertain to what extent the BBC would participate, and what the cost would be. Greene made available thirty-two hours a week of prime broadcasting time, despite the misgivings of many of his staff, and produced a professional costing for the whole operation. He was intensely proud of the role he played in the founding of the Open University, which later awarded him an honorary degree.

Greene's period as Director-General also saw much change and controversy. The Greene years saw many inhibitions and taboos cast aside. For many they were the heyday of BBC television programming: *Steptoe and Son*, *Till Death Us Do Part*, The Wednesday Play, *Cathy Come Home*, *The Forsyte Saga*, *Civilisation* and the early satire programmes such as *That Was The Week That Was*. There were many international plaudits.

Others, particularly Mrs Mary Whitehouse, tended to regard Greene as the cloven-hoofed begetter of the permissive society, responsible for the erosion of standards of morality. Greene himself felt that the questioning of established values and the puncturing of hypocrisy were healthy instincts, vital in a flourishing democracy. I once discussed with him the problem raised by pre-recorded interviews where a politician wished to excise something that he had said, realising that he had inadvertently let the cat out of the bag. Greene's comment was: 'It is the job of broadcasting to winkle cats out of bags.'

Hugh Greene generally enjoyed a good relationship with his Board of Governors, especially with his first Chairman, Sir Arthur fforde, a former headmaster of Rugby School. The only serious complaints from the Board, particularly from the Vice-Chairman, Sir James Duff, arose as a result of last-minute smutty additions to *That Was The Week That Was*.

Greene did not wish to risk Duff's resignation and later

declared: 'It was in my capacity as a subversive anarchist that I yielded to the enormous pressure of my fellow subversives and put *That Was The Week That Was* on the air, and it was as a pillar of the Establishment that I yielded to the fascist hyena-like howls to take it off again.'

After fforde's successor, Lord Normanbrook, died in mid-June 1967, the Prime Minister, Harold Wilson, transferred Lord Hill overnight from the chairmanship of the Independent Television Authority to that of the BBC, with the evident intention of getting rid of Greene (see Hill, p. 258). The Director-General had no great respect for his new chairman and their relationship was noticeably cool. Before the end of the year 1967 Greene had to tell Hill that he was about to be divorced for the second time. It was generally felt that two divorces for a BBC Director-General were too many, and Greene decided to resign.

Lord Hill was therefore presented on a plate with what Harold Wilson had apparently wanted. But Hill wished to make it publicly clear that he was not responsible for Greene's departure. The chosen way of doing this, which the late William Clark, the former Public Relations Adviser to Sir Anthony Eden, claimed to have suggested, was to have Greene appointed as a BBC Governor shortly after his retirement.

It was a role which Reith had hungered for but had been denied. Few people, other than Greene and Hill, thought it a good idea, and it was awkward for Greene's successor, Charles Curran. After less than two years Greene had had enough of the BBC Board and resigned.

In retirement Hugh Greene reverted to the two great loves of his life: books and foreign affairs. He became the chairman of Bodley Head, the firm which published his brother Graham. With Graham he wrote *The Spy's Bedside Book* and, on his own, two books about the literary rivals of

Sherlock Holmes. He also became the owner of a second-hand bookshop.

Greene advised the governments of Greece and Israel on broadcasting matters and made several documentary films about his days in broadcasting, some in German. He became a lonely figure after the death of his third wife, a former German cabaret star, but his last years were made happy by his marriage to Sarah Grahame, an Australian he met at a Commonwealth Broadcasting Conference in New Zealand.

Sir Hugh Greene had great charm, combined with a strong streak of mischief. He was often aloof and he could be ruthless. He was a very private man who made a great contribution to broadcasting.

12
Gilbert Harding

*'Mr Harding is somewhat of an
eccentric.'*

Gilbert Charles Harding, born Hereford 5 June 1907, unmarried; schoolmaster, lecturer and police constable; correspondent in Cyprus for The Times; *BBC Monitoring Service 1940, Assistant, Outside Broadcasts Department,* The Microphone Wants to Know 1942, *Assistant to Canadian Representative 1944–47, freelance performer on radio* Round Britain Quiz, The Brains Trust, Twenty Questions, *and on television* What's My Line?, Harding Finds Out, I Know What I Like, Who Said That? *1947–60,; publications* Treasury of Insult *1952,* Along My Line *1953,* Book of Manners *1958,* A Book of Happiness *1959; died London, 16 November 1960, aged 53.*

In the 1950s the biggest household name in television was undoubtedly Gilbert Harding. Millions switched on *What's My Line?* every Sunday in fascinated anticipation of what new example of outrageous behaviour this irascible man might produce. He was arrogant and rude. He bullied people shamelessly. As like as not he would be the worse for alcohol, and he was prone to lose his temper. Yet he had great personal charm and a very well-stocked mind.

I first had dealings with Gilbert Harding when I went to America at the end of the war as the BBC's Washington news correspondent. He was then working in Toronto as the Assistant to the BBC's Canadian Representative. He did various broadcasting jobs such as choosing suitable Canadians to take part in the hour-long Commonwealth radio hookup which used to precede the annual Christmas Day broadcast by the Monarch. He also had to do a certain amount of public relations work for the BBC, for which he was perhaps not the ideal choice.

The Canadian Broadcasting Corporation kindly provided him with an office in their headquarters in Jarvis Street, which was also the brothel street of Toronto. Gilbert, who was homosexual, rented some comfortable rooms there, not minding his flamboyant neighbours. Shortly afterwards he was at a dinner party when a pompous Toronto lady asked him where he was living. He told her he had found rooms in Jarvis Street. 'That's not a very fashionable address,' she said. 'Neither is Toronto, madam,' Harding replied – a remark which thirty years later I found was still remembered there.

Gilbert Harding liked to make regular visits across the border to the BBC's office in New York. To get an American visa in those days you had to fill up an enormously long application form which ended with the question designed to trap Comintern agents into perjury: 'Is it your intention to overthrow the lawful government of the United States by force and violence?' – or words to that effect. Gilbert is said to have written on one occasion, 'Sole object of journey'. I can't vouch for the truth of that. He was the sort of person about whom many apocryphal stories were told. However, it was certainly in character.

He had led a restless and unsatisfying life. He was born in 1907 in the workhouse at Hereford where his father was the master and his mother the matron. Gilbert's father died when he was only 3. His mother, to whom he was deeply devoted, managed to get him into the Royal Orphanage School, from which he won a scholarship to Queen's College, Cambridge. He played a considerable part in the debates at the Cambridge Union. Sir Arthur Conan Doyle and G. K. Chesterton were two of the visiting celebrities with whom he debated. Chesterton became a kind of mentor to Harding and correctly forecast that he would eventually become a Roman Catholic.

He left Cambridge with a third class degree and a fair number of debts to local tradesmen. He studied theology briefly at the Community of the Resurrection at Mirfield in Yorkshire, and then Roman Catholic doctrine at the Benedictine Abbey at Belmont, near Hereford. He was duly received into the Roman Catholic Church and afterwards held teaching jobs in many different boys' schools in England, Canada and France.

At one point he had a brief and not particularly successful spell as a policeman in Bradford before accepting an offer from the Cambridge University Appointments Board of a job in Cyprus teaching English, first to the Greek community and later to the Turks. He also became the stringer correspondent for *The Times* but failed to gain a place on its staff when he returned to London. He got desultory employment at a crammer's, and decided to become a barrister. He began to eat his dinners at Gray's Inn and was preparing for the bar finals when war broke out and he abruptly abandoned the law.

In 1939 Harding was 32 and not due to be called up for some time. He was not keen to go into the ranks. As he put it, 'Having earned my living being violently offensive and sarcastic to young men who I knew would now be captains and majors only too glad to get their own back,

I decided that it would have to be a commission or nothing.' For a while it was to be nothing, and then another dreary teaching job at a crammer's. Suddenly his fortune changed. He received an offer from the BBC to join its new Monitoring Service.

In the summer of 1939, when Maurice Latey and I were running the BBC's small German News Talks section, we were asked to listen daily to one of the Nazi news bulletins and to circulate a brief note to the newsrooms about what they were broadcasting. As war approached, and particularly after it started, this task was greatly expanded to become a professional operation with a large number of skilled monitors including George Weidenfeld, recording and translating what was being broadcast by the Axis powers not only in German and Italian but in all languages. They were also able to pick up much of the internal communications within the enemy countries.

The Monitoring Service was evacuated to a mansion at Wood Norton, near Evesham, which had been built by the exiled Duke of Orleans after the French Revolution and was heavily decorated with fleurs-de-lis. Its reports were teleprinted to Broadcasting House where a team of subeditors compiled a *Daily Digest of Foreign Broadcasts* which went to various service departments as well as to the BBC newsrooms.

Harding was one of this team. After Broadcasting House was bombed he, too, was moved to Evesham and worked on the Cabinet Report, a special analysis which went straight to the War Cabinet. Sometimes he would be telephoned directly by Churchill who once asked, when Gilbert was on leave, 'Where is that man with the succinct mind?'

Gilbert's monitoring job at Evesham was interesting, but he craved a more active life, and in 1942 he moved to the Outside Broadcasts Department where he shared an office with Raymond Glendenning. He developed his broadcasting technique through recording interviews which were beamed to North America. Under the title *The Microphone Wants to Know* he also made many short radio features about various aspects of wartime life on the home front. After two years he applied for the newly created post in Toronto.

On his return from Canada Harding became a freelance. During the war there had been a popular radio programme *Transatlantic Quiz*, a general knowledge contest between a team in London and one in New York. The BBC had to abandon it in the post-war period for lack of dollars. But the format was converted into *Round Britain Quiz* with Lionel Hale posing the questions in London and Gilbert Harding as the peripatetic regional quizmaster. He also presented another radio panel game, *Twenty Questions*, and became the chairman of the revived wartime favourite, the *Brains Trust*. He performed well and they all had large followings.

What's My Line? was one of the American television programmes for which the danceband leader Maurice Winnick had shrewdly acquired the British rights. It was popular partly because it brought a succession of ordinary members of the public before the cameras, which no other show did at that time (it was first broadcast from Lime Grove in 1951).

Its other strength was the panel's mixture of contrasted and complementary personalities. The standard pattern seemed to be an actress with a lot of charm but a somewhat fey manner, a good-looking, elegant, intellectual lady, someone in showbusiness who was entertaining but not too bright, and Mr Grumpy himself played from the start by Gilbert Harding. When I first watched it the others were Barbara Kelly, Isobel Barnett and David Nixon. They all wore evening dress, as did their producer, T. Leslie Jackson, who collected an allowance of £5 every week for doing so.

Viewers were not really all that interested in whether the panel would correctly identify the sagger maker's bottom knocker or whatever other esoteric occupation was pursued by a challenger. They were waiting to see how soon Gilbert Harding's temper would explode, as it nearly always did, especially if the person he was interrogating employed a coy circumlocution or misused the English language. He was a verbal sadist. He used to refer to himself as a 'telephoney'.

Despite the embarrassment he often caused Gilbert Harding did not lack support in the upper ranges of the BBC. Sir Ian Jacob replied to one complaining correspondent:

Mr Harding is somewhat of an eccentric and there are times when his attitude and bearing go beyond what is proper even in a light entertainment programme; but his characteristics are well-known, and on balance it seems to me better to have someone who, though he may occasionally annoy and irritate, can also stimulate, rather than fall back on a flat level of boring propriety.

Some of us tried hard to find some role for Harding that was worthy of his abilities. In my department we offered him a run of six programmes investigating complaints submitted by viewers. It was entitled *Harding Finds Out* and was produced by Huw Wheldon, but it never really got off the ground. Cecil McGivern, a fellow Catholic and close friend of Harding, sent me one of his acerbic comments: 'I shall be glad when this series is over. It should be called "Harding Matters".' Two other series designed to exploit his egocentric personality and his well-stocked mind were *I Know What I Like* and *Who Said That?*.

Much has been written about the famous *Face to Face* interview with John Freeman who was rather unjustly accused of deliberately making Gilbert cry. What happened was this: the producer kept the guest always in shot. Freeman's face was not shown, though sometimes the back of his neck was. Often there was a very tight picture of just the top half of the guest's face. *Face to Face* was normally broadcast live on Sundays, alternating fortnightly with *Monitor. What's My Line?* was also live on Sundays, so the interview had to be pre-recorded, one of the very few in the series that was. It was also one of the very few times that Freeman slipped up on the meticulous homework he normally undertook in preparation for these programmes. He was intending to hint at Harding's homosexuality, not a subject you could openly mention in the 1950s. He knew that Harding had not served in the armed forces during the war. Overtly homosexual men were not normally called up. Freeman was intending to approach indirectly the question of whether Harding had served by first asking whether he had ever seen anyone die.

Freeman did not know that Harding's hard-working and disappointed mother had died the week before, with her son at her side. Tears began to well up in his eyes, which were clearly seen by viewers on the tight close-up picture. Freeman did not immediately notice the distress he was causing. As soon as he did, he veered off on to a quite different subject.

Harding himself asked to see the recording with the producer before it was transmitted. He had mentioned his sister, and was worried lest he had said something derogatory about her. He had no complaint to make about the question concerning dying, which caused such distress to his many friends when it came to be transmitted. Harding also defended Freeman from those who thought he had been a sadistic interrogator. John Freeman himself said that it was the question he most regretted asking on *Face to Face*.

Gilbert could be a kind friend and a stimulating companion. The programme with Freeman had shown that in addition to being brusque and bad-tempered he was a lonely and unhappy man. He was aware that he dissipated his talents through drink. Aged only 53, he dropped dead in 1960 outside Broadcasting House, while waiting for a taxi after he had recorded an edition of *Round Britain Quiz*. He was Britain's first television personality.

13

Tahu Hole

'We are keeping very, very calm.'

Tahu Ronald Charles Pearce Hole, CBE 1956, born 29 March 1908, married Joyce Margaret Wingate (died 1986); journalist New Zealand and Australia 1926–37. London correspondent and war correspondent, Sydney Morning Herald *1937–40;* BBC *commentator 1940–41, joined Overseas Service 1941, producer,* War Review *1942–43, Overseas Talks Manager 1944, Assistant Editor, News Division, and Member of Editorial Board 1949, Editor, News 1948, Director of Administration 1958–60; one of the founders of British Commonwealth International Newsfilm Agency Ltd (later Visnews, still later Reuters Television) 1956, deputy chairman 1957, chairman 1958; editorial board of Royal Institute of International Affairs 1949–54; died 22 November 1985, aged 77.*

If the rest of this book concerns people who in their different ways helped to create the reputation of the BBC, here, as what is known in television as a cutaway shot, is one who did much to destroy it.

Tahu Hole was a New Zealander. He was not, as some supposed, a Maori, though Tahu was the Maori name for a piece of land owned by his family. It also means lover or spouse. He was a tall, massive man with jowls like a bloodhound, who usually wore a black Homburg hat and a long overcoat. He studied journalism in Christchurch, worked as a reporter on various New Zealand and Australian papers, became the news editor of the *Sydney Morning Herald* and in 1937 came to London as the correspondent of that newspaper.

Hole let it be known that he had been the lover, no doubt the last lover, of Margot Asquith. I cannot vouch for the truth of this claim, but her final volume of memoirs, published in 1943 when she was 79, is dedicated to a small group of men 'whose friendship and affection', she wrote, 'have been a pleasure to me since the war was declared'. One of those named was Tahu Hole, who was then 35. He used to boast of his sexual prowess and elderly ladies seemed to be fascinated by him. The Countess of Abingdon and Lindsey, who died in October 1978 at the age of 82, left more than £1.5 million to Tahu Hole and his wife. Her bequest at last prompted *Who's Who* to consider him worth an entry, although he was then 70 and had been retired from the BBC Board of Management for almost two decades.

After the outbreak of war Hole used BBC studios to beam broadcasts to the Antipodes. Fairly soon he was engaged as a regular news commentator on the Overseas Service, and he joined the staff in 1943, working on Overseas Talks. After the war Sir William Haley established a small editorial board, of which he was himself Editor-in-Chief, to co-ordinate the domestic and overseas output of news in a combined News Division. Patrick Ryan, the Editor, News, was the head of the joint operation. He was a vivacious journalist trained on the *Manchester Guardian* and the *Daily Telegraph*. His deputy was Jim Macgregor who before the war had been an announcer in Scotland. Overseas News was represented by its Editor, Bernard

Moore, and his Talks deputy, Tahu Hole, the most junior of the four.

In 1947, through a series of unconnected events, this arrangement collapsed. Ryan joined *The Times* as assistant editor, with the hope of one day becoming editor. Moore was selected to go to New York as the BBC's first United Nations correspondent. Macgregor fell seriously ill. This was how Tahu Hole came to be promoted by Haley into a post that was well beyond his capabilities. BBC news at that time was respected throughout the world. Hole thought he could maintain that reputation by following a line of extreme caution. Insecure, and uncertain in his news judgement, he ran the News Division on a policy of safety first. There must never be a mistake, no matter how slow and pedestrian the bulletins were, and all items broadcast must be supported by at least two sources.

Anthony Wigan, who was Foreign News Editor under Hole, commented:

There was a good deal of dishonesty in carrying out the new policy. Hole knew quite well, and so did Haley, that nearly all Reuters' Western Hemisphere stuff was straight Associated Press. Yet the two agencies were regarded as legitimate confirmation of each other under the absurd 'two agency' rule. Bob Stimson [the BBC's former Rome correspondent] told me much later that he always went down the road to the A.P. office with any exclusive story in Rome; the walk back gave them time to file before he did – and that, of course, was regarded as confirmation too.

Gerald Priestland, foreign correspondent in many different countries before becoming religious affairs correspondent (see Priestland, p. 215), made a similar criticism of Hole's edict in his autobiography *Something Understood:*

Information from a reliable source would be held back until a less reliable source had caught up with it. Often it was known that the two agencies which appeared to confirm one another were actually the same man in the field. When I became a foreign correspondent myself I learnt that if I got an exclusive story the only way to get it on the air was to give a carbon copy to my competitor from Reuters, even at the expense of being thought soft in the head by him.

This new policy of course deprecated any attempt to obtain scoop interviews. Guy Hadley, who was the BBC's correspondent in Athens when Hole took over as Editor, News, recalled how he obtained an exclusive interview with Queen Frederica on relief work in the Greek villages and another with Marshal Papagos, the Prime Minister, on the Greek government's struggle to defeat the Communist threat. Hadley commented: 'I hoped, not unnaturally, that my London Office would be pleased. Not so. They sent me an angry letter of censure, deprived me of a salary increase, and sternly forbade me to seek such interviews in future.'

To quote Gerald Priestland again:

Amongst his staff he [Hole] inspired nothing but terror, exuding a sinister aroma of power as if he knew something to the discredit of each one of them, as I suppose he took care to do. The only people with countervailing knowledge, and who were therefore immune to his terror, were the Paris and New York correspondents. From time to time Tahu would arrive in their territories 'on a tour of inspection', enjoy a hearty dinner with them at the best restaurants (he was partial to red snapper) and then vanish into the girlie-show district with his black homburg at a rakish angle. Two or three days later he would reappear in the correspondent's office, badly hung over and asking to have his flight home confirmed.

The New York correspondent mentioned was F. D.

Walker, who later served with distinction in Bonn. The man in Paris was the most illustrious of the BBC's first corps of foreign correspondents, Thomas Cadett. On one occasion Hole went to Paris to tell Cadett that the BBC was going to reduce his overseas living allowance. Hole put his arm round Cadett's shoulders in a bear-like embrace and said ingratiatingly, 'Remember, Tom, I'm your brother.' Cadett's reply was terse: 'Cain, I presume.'

My most vivid experience of Hole's insecure news judgement was at the start of the Korean war. I was then the Washington correspondent. It was before there was news on television and I beamed my daily radio dispatches over a regular transatlantic circuit at 5.45 p.m. London time, just before lunchtime in Washington. They were recorded in Broadcasting House, quarried for use in the news bulletins at 6 p.m. and 9 p.m. and usually broadcast in voice in *Radio News Reel* on the Light Programme at 7 p.m. This daily circuit had only a one-way line between Washington and New York, which meant that when I spoke to London they could not speak to me.

Early in 1948, shortly before Hole took over as Editor, News, all we BBC foreign correspondents had been sent detailed instructions on what to do when major news broke and it was likely that a live insert into a news bulletin would be required. This followed the assassination of Mahatma Gandhi on 30 January. Robert Stimson, then the BBC correspondent in India, had been standing only yards away from Gandhi when he was shot. His vivid eyewitness account was being recorded at the music studios in Maida Vale while the six o'clock news was being broadcast, yet there was no way at that time of diverting the Delhi circuit to Broadcasting House. The drill we had been sent was designed to prevent a repetition of such a missed opportunity.

The North Koreans invaded South Korea on 25 June 1950. President Truman flew back from Missouri to Washington to confer with his Secretaries of State and Defense. For a day and a half there was intense military and diplomatic activity. The Security Council had called upon members of the United Nations for help in forcing the invaders to withdraw.

On the morning of 27 June I received a telephone call from the White House inviting me to a special press conference. Truman was known to be conferring with the Congressional leaders and it was obvious that something major was happening. So I quickly put the live insert drill into action. I extended the circuit to cover the 6 p.m. news, booked a second line from New York so that I could converse with London and would be able to hear the newsreader's cue, and cabled all this information to the News Division.

At the White House, while Truman was still closeted with the Congressional leaders, his press secretary gave us copies of a statement in Palmerstonian prose setting out the steps that the American Commander-in-Chief had taken to meet the situation posed by the invasion of South Korea. Truman had ordered American air and sea forces to give the Korean government troops cover and support. He had also taken action to protect Formosa, the Philippines and Indo-China, in response to the call from the Security Council.

I walked from the White House to the studio, with a number of British newsmen who were all discussing the significance of the news we had just been handed, and how it was going to lead in their newspapers the next day. I got to the studio with just enough time to write a short lead summarising the action that Truman was taking, and then intended to read the President's short historic statement in full.

I checked with the Foreign Duty Editor, George Tonkin, that they wanted me to come live into the 6 p.m. news. He told me that Hole did not wish me to do so. Instead Hole would like me to come live into the 9 p.m. news with 'considered reactions' to the announcement. He was afraid that a live announcement from the place where the news had just broken might cause a panic, and in Britain people were keeping 'very, very calm'. Tonkin also said that Hole thought 'the North Koreans might retire'. I begged Tonkin to persuade Hole (who could hear this conversation) to come and speak to me himself. But Hole refused. I lost my temper and made over the circuit some pejorative remarks about the unprofessional way the news was being run, which Hole never forgave.

Three years later I gave up my eight-year Washington assignment. By then I was one of the senior foreign correspondents and I was hoping for a job at home so that my children might have a British education. Cecil McGivern, the Television Programme Controller, had for long been keen that the television service should start its own service of daily news in vision, in addition to the *Television Newsreel*. But this was not to be. In April 1953 the Director-General, Sir Ian Jacob, announced, 'As it is not practicable to separate the responsibility for News from responsibility for Newsreels, both will be included in the service for which News Division will be responsible.' McGivern's nose was badly out of joint because George Barnes, the Director of Television, had not consulted him before surrendering the creation of news on television, and the control of the existing *Television Newsreel*, to Tahu Hole.

Having been much involved with television news in America, I hoped to have some hand in this new venture. However, Hole clearly did not want me around. He told me that I was so out of touch with things British that I would first have to serve for at least two years as a junior subeditor (dropping a couple of BBC salary grades) before I could be considered for any domestic news post. I must either continue as a foreign correspondent – and he offered me South Africa, saying that my children could get an English type of education there – or I must go on the redundant pool. I opted for potential redundancy. Fortunately it did not come to that. Immediately after my return home I was appointed to be Head of the Television Talks Department which dealt with current affairs and the other factual programmes.

It took more than a year after Jacob's announcement before Hole's *News and Newsreel* went on the air, in July 1954, and a sorry amateurish mess it was. When no appropriate newsfilm was available the announcer, out of vision, read the news against captions in order that the integrity of the news should not be sullied by what was called 'the cult of personality', through showing the reader's face. Indeed it was only a few weeks before the start of Independent Television News on 22 September 1955 that Hole conceded that the faces of Richard Baker, Robert Dougall and Kenneth Kendall, the newsreaders, might actually be seen.

The public reaction to Hole's *News and Newsreel* was far from enthusiastic. The *Star* said that it was 'about as impressive visually as the fat stock prices'. Lionel Gamlin, a former BBC announcer, described it in *The Spectator* as a 'lamentably non-telegenic presentation of television news' that was 'at once singularly clumsy and unrealistic', and Gerald Barry, the former editor of the *News Chronicle*, said it must have sent Norman Collins and his friends in the new commercial television companies down to the cellar for a bottle of champagne.

In 1958 Hole pressed Jacob hard to give him a seat on the Board of Management. The Director-General, who had belatedly come to recognise Hole's news inadequacies, decided to appoint Hugh Carleton Greene as Director of News and Current Affairs, and to move Hole to become Director of Administration in Greene's place. Jacob made certain, however, that the responsibility for handling staff matters should not be entrusted to Hole but to a newly created Director of Staff Administration. Greene himself described Hole's News Division as 'the Kremlin of the BBC'.

After Hole was moved, BBC Television News at last seriously started to compete with ITN. Donald Edwards, who had successfully run the important news operation at Bush House for many years, was appointed as the new Editor, and staff morale throughout the News Division was transformed. Where Hole had conducted a running skirmish with the television service, Edwards immediately set about making peace. He applied to attend the weekly meeting of the television controllers – White City's cabinet – and persuaded the Director of Television to lend him three of his best producers to examine what was needed to improve the news service. Edwards accepted their frankly expressed strictures, and his deputy Stuart Hood, also from Bush House, implemented their suggested reforms at Alexandra Palace. One of Hood's innovations was to employ Nan Winton, previously one of our *Panorama* reporters, as the BBC's first woman television news reader.

When Greene became Director-General in 1960 one of his first actions was to persuade the Governors to approve a golden handshake for Hole so that he might be retired early. A press announcement issued on 15 March 1960 said that Hole's decision to resign at the age of 51 was influenced by 'his desire to develop his other interests while still comparatively young'. Some wondered what the 'other interests' might be. He was, in fact, angling for a post with the Independent Television Authority.

The Committee on the Future of Broadcasting headed by Sir Harry Pilkington had just been formed. One of its tasks was to recommend whether the franchise for a further television channel should be awarded to the BBC or to ITV. Greene's Board of Management carefully considered its tactics in relation to the Pilkington Committee. A top secret document was produced which drew attention to the financial involvement of much of the national and local press in commercial television companies. It pointed out that there was already a dangerous concentration of the control of information in too few hands and proposed that the BBC should draw public attention to the vested interests behind much of the press campaign in favour of the ITV.

The Chairman of the ITA, Sir Ivone Kirkpatrick, meeting Hugh Greene on some social occasion, complained about this BBC tactic. Greene was privately disturbed that the document must have been leaked. On his return to Broadcasting House he recalled all the numbered copies, which had gone only to the members of the Board of Management. (This was before the days of photocopying.) The paper that had been issued to the Director of Administration was missing.

Greene invited Hole, by then retired, to come to Broadcasting House, without indicating why he wanted to see him. When Hole arrived at the 'Third Floor Front', the Director-General put it to him that before leaving he had deliberately leaked the paper to independent television. Flustered, Hole said that he had taken the paper home to read; his neighbour and old friend Norman Collins had dropped by unexpectedly to see him; he, Hole, had been called away to the telephone and Collins must have picked it up off his desk and pocketed it. Greene, from whose lips I heard this account, recalled: 'I said "Tahu, I do not believe a word of this farrago. Get out of here, and never darken these doors again!" And he went out of my office blubbing.' Greene added to me that he sorely regretted not knowing about the leak when he recommended the golden handshake.

14

Grace Wyndham Goldie

'A whim of iron'

Grace Murrell Nisbet, OBE 1958, born 26 March 1900, married 1928 Frank Wyndham Goldie, actor (died 1957), no children; history mistress, Brighton and Hove High School 1925–28; in Liverpool as (a) playreader to Liverpool Repertory Theatre, (b) Workers' Educational Association lecturer, (c) examiner in history for the Northern Universities Joint Board 1928–34; in London as drama and entertainment critic of The Listener *1934–41 (1936–39 also television critic); Board of Trade, Senior Assistant, Consumer Needs Department 1942–44; BBC radio talks producer 1944, television talks producer 1948, Assistant Head of Talks, Television 1954, Head of Talks and Current Affairs, Television 1962, Head of Talks and Current Affairs Group, Television 1963; retired 1965; publication* Facing the Nation – Television and Politics 1936–76 (1977); *died 3 June 1986, aged 86.*

Grace Wyndham Goldie's name is legendary in television history as the founder of current affairs and political programmes, and as *The Listener*'s first professional television reviewer. She was born in Scotland in 1900 when Queen Victoria was still on the throne. Her father, R. J. Nisbet, was a civil engineer who helped build the spectacular

West Highland railway and many bridges and roads in the Inverness area. She always had a high regard and respect for engineers.

Mr Nisbet's work took him to Egypt, and Grace attended a French convent school in Alexandria. She was 16 when the family returned to Britain and settled near Cheltenham. Grace spent a year at Cheltenham Ladies' College where she was told that she had no hope of getting into a British university because of her flawed early education abroad. That kind of an assertion was bound to be challenged by Grace. Indeed one of the best ways of persuading her to take some course of action was to suggest that it could not be done.

Using her own initiative she managed to get a place at Bristol University and achieved a first class degree in History. From there she went on to Somerville College, Oxford, where she got a second in Modern Greats, the new faculty of Politics, Philosophy and Economics. In the first quarter of the twentieth century it was still something of an achievement for a woman to attend a university, let alone two. For the next three years she taught history at a girls' high school in Brighton.

Grace was attractive, petite, bird-like and very feminine. At the age of 28, she married Frank Wyndham Goldie, a handsome actor who for stage purposes called himself simply Wyndham Goldie. Where he dropped a name, she added one, liking to be known professionally as Grace Wyndham Goldie.

For six years the Goldies lived in Liverpool where Frank acted and directed at the Repertory Company. Grace used to read plays for the theatre and eventually wrote a book on its history. She also lectured on drama for the Workers' Educational Association and examined in history for the Northern Universities Joint Board.

They moved to London in 1934. Rex Lambert, the first editor of *The Listener*, had met Grace in Liverpool and was struck by her clarity of mind. He invited her to write regular criticism for him, first of radio drama and entertainment, and, after 1936, of television. When war closed down television she reverted to regular radio reviewing for *The Listener* and wrote articles for the *Radio Times*. She worked for two years in the Board of Trade.

In August 1944 Mrs Goldie joined the BBC staff as a radio talks producer, in the vacancy created when Guy Burgess managed to get himself transferred to the Foreign Office. She soon established her ability to cope with major projects such as a series on atomic energy in 1947 and *Challenge of Our Time* in 1948. That same year she was appointed a producer in the Television Talks Department headed by Mary Adams, although Bertrand Russell gave her his considered opinion: 'Television will be of no importance in your lifetime or mine.'

At Alexandra Palace Grace produced many major programmes about international affairs and politics. One series was *Foreign Correspondent* using Edward Ward and that splendid Australian war correspondent Chester Wilmot, who was killed in the crash of a Comet while flying back from a filming trip in the Far East. Another was *International Commentary* with Christopher Mayhew.

She found that politicians who had held junior office, but had lost their seats at a General Election and suddenly found time on their hands, made good television presenters for the programmes she wished to mount. In the early 1950s the men she chose tended to be right-wing socialists who subsequently all left the Labour Party, such as Aidan Crawley and Woodrow Wyatt, as well as Mayhew himself. Grace's own political instincts were conservative. Frank Goldie used to work part-time for the

Conservative Central Office, and she was a close friend of Earl Woolton, the chairman of the Tory Party.

She also had the drive and resourcefulness to mount the mammoth election results programmes, starting in 1950. She enlisted the help of academics such as David Butler and Robert McKenzie. Leading politicians were slowly persuaded to appear on television in such programmes as *Press Conference*, although most preferred the larger audiences and national coverage that radio then provided.

At Alexandra Palace Mrs Goldie was finding it difficult to work with her head of department, Mrs Mary Adams, so she set up a semi-autonomous current affairs unit in the Marylebone Road with three bright young men she had recruited: James Bredin, Michael Peacock and Geoffrey Johnson Smith.

In 1953 Grace went to the United States on a three-month scholarship awarded by the State Department to study relations between politics and the American media. She came to Washington where I was finishing my term as news correspondent and I was able to take her to press conferences at the White House and various government agencies, and to introduce her to the people who covered Washington activities on television. She was impressed by the speed with which film of a news conference we had attended one afternoon could be broadcast early that evening. There was no videotape then, but the Americans had very quick film processing. However, she was scornful of its picture quality. The composition of the images on the television screen, and the impact they made were, to her, more important than journalistic enterprise and topicality.

Mary Adams, Head of the Television Talks Department, was made an assistant to Cecil McGivern and both Grace and I were candidates to succeed her. We attended an appointments board just before Christmas 1953. When I was told I had been selected I was asked, doubtless because they were concerned at my lack of television production experience, whether I was prepared to have Grace as the Assistant Head of the Department. No such post had hitherto existed. I immediately agreed. Had I known her better, I should have hesitated, for it was contrary to Grace's nature to be assistant head of anything. She had to be totally in charge of whatever activity she was engaged in, which did not make her a natural deputy. Moreover, her personality was a difficult one. Sir Ian Trethowan, the former Director-General, wrote in his autobiography *Split Screen*, 'Her sharp tongue and angry, snapping eyes were feared and disliked by newer and more junior members of her staff, but the older hands held her in deep respect, even awe.' It was a common saying in the television service that Grace had a whim of iron. She tended to claim personal credit for other people's achievements and found it difficult to keep appointments on time.

Within a few weeks of my appointment, Television Talks, which was then the Cinderella of the programme departments, moved from Alexandra Palace and Marylebone Road to Lime Grove. We were the last department to do so. As my own expertise was in politics and international affairs, there was no point in maintaining a separate current affairs unit, and Grace and I divided between us the responsibility for supervising individual programmes in this area, which were the ones most liable to get the BBC into trouble.

I also soon discovered that the best way of using Grace's outstanding professional abilities was to put her in total charge of specific activities, such as arranging the training programmes for new staff. McGivern kept calling for more output from Television Talks. We became a sought-after department for radio producers on training attachment to television and as the output increased the department expanded steadily.

When there was a new programme series to be started, the revitalised *Panorama* or *Tonight* or *Monitor* for example, I put her in charge of its launch, for she would apply her own very high standards of production integrity and she would fight like a tiger for the necessary resources, which were always in short supply. But when the new programme was up and running it was essential to move Grace on to some fresh enterprise on which to exercise her intellectual vigour, because she tended to interfere with every programme detail and seemed incapable of managing people, especially women, on a loose rein.

It was also important that she should continue to produce major programmes herself. One of these was to celebrate Sir Winston Churchill's eightieth birthday on 30 November 1954. Sir Ian Jacob, who had remained close to Churchill, was insistent that we should not make a programme that would look like a preview of an obituary. Richard Cawston and Donald Baverstock were working with Grace on this project, and it was Donald who had the bright idea of making the programme one in which several of Churchill's friends, representing the different facets of his very full life, would give their birthday greetings directly to him by addressing the camera lens, while the television audience eavesdropped. That would be a programme *for* him, not one *about* him, and could not look like an obituary.

We agreed that Lord Ismay, then the Secretary-General of NATO, would be the ideal person to present the programme and I flew to Paris to enlist his co-operation.

He immediately agreed and added that what Churchill really loved was a surprise. He urged us to seek the support of Lady Churchill and the Prime Minister's private secretaries but otherwise to keep the whole idea a secret.

I then asked him to suggest which people should represent the various services. Who did Churchill like best? Ismay was blunt and most helpful. As far as the army was concerned, certainly not Field-Marshal Lord Alanbrooke, the former Chief of the Imperial General Staff. Churchill's favourite soldier, he said, was Lord Freyberg, the New Zealand VC whose name had been a byword for heroism in the First World War.

Who for the Navy? I asked. Well, not Mountbatten, was the immediate reply. Much better would be Admiral Sir Philip Vian, the man who had sailed the *Cossack* into the territorial waters of neutral Norway on Churchill's orders in February 1940. With the cry 'The Navy is here!' he had rescued 300 British merchant seamen who were being taken to Germany as prisoners in the *Altmark*.

I relayed his suggestions to Grace and set about organising the programme. Lady Churchill and the private secretaries gladly agreed to keep it a secret from Sir Winston. The transmission was to be from seven to seven-thirty, just before a family dinner party at 10 Downing Street. Grace arranged with Rab Butler, the Chancellor of the Exchequer, that the Churchill party could go through the communicating door to watch the programme in 11 Downing Street, where Huw Wheldon would have a 'Roving Eye' outside broadcast camera for the Prime Minister to reply if he wished. It was merely billed in the *Radio Times* as *Birthday Greetings to Sir Winston Churchill from Some of his Friends*, without any details of the celebrities

141

taking part, who included several Commonwealth Prime Ministers.

Some of Churchill's official family, such as his personal secretary, his detective and the policeman normally outside the door of No 10, were to be with Ismay in the studio to give their greetings live. Many of the others, having duly been warned to keep the secret, came to Lime Grove to be filmed beforehand. When Admiral Vian arrived for his filming session he said to Grace, 'I was having lunch at the In and Out today and found myself sitting next to Alanbrooke. I said to him, "Are you taking part in this television thing for Churchill's birthday?" He told me he hadn't been invited.' Grace said icily, 'We did ask you to keep it a secret.' Vian replied, 'Oh, you can always trust Brookey anywhere.'

Grace went to Paris for a further talk with Lord Ismay, and various other friends of Churchill such as Lady Violet Bonham Carter were duly filmed. The secret was kept, almost too well, for shortly before the programme we heard that the Queen had decided to give Sir Winston a personal birthday present and had invited him to Buckingham Palace for a drink at seven o'clock, before his family dinner party but just as Grace's elaborate programme was due to begin. I urgently telephoned one of the private secretaries at No 10 and admired the smooth way the Establishment old boy network went into action. In next to no time we heard that the Queen's invitation had been changed to five o'clock.

The programme went off well. Huw Wheldon reported that Churchill was very tired and he did not know whether he would speak. Grace, watching the preview monitor in the Lime Grove production gallery, saw him slowly shake his head and shed a tear when Lady Violet said that courage was what he had given to his friends and to the country. But at the end, after Lord Ismay and the others in the studio had toasted him in 'practical' champagne (i.e. not cold tea laced with soda water, as served in television plays) he suddenly came to life and made an elegantly worded extempore response, thanking his cherished friends for their friendly greetings.

It was Churchill's first and last live television appearance, and it was one of Grace's last major personal productions, with the exception of three mammoth General Election results programmes which she masterminded before she retired in 1965, well beyond the normal BBC retiring age. In 1962 she succeeded me as Head of Television Talks, which included documentaries and all kinds of factual programmes. The following year what had been a unified department was divided into four, with Grace as a kind of Group Head Emeritus.

Frank Goldie had died in 1957. They had had no children, and Grace found relaxation difficult. Rather than face an empty flat she tended to stay on late at Lime Grove, holding post-mortems on the talks programmes which had been broadcast that evening. Emboldened in the hospitality room, she would tell leading politicians what she thought of their television performances in the same acerbic terms as she was wont to use to the junior producers, the 'bright young men' who were her substitute children. These occasions sadly diminished her reputation.

For two years after her retirement Grace Wyndham Goldie was an associate member of Nuffield College, Oxford, where she wrote *Facing the Nation*, one of the best books about the relationship between television and politics, in which she had played such an important pioneering role. Though not a Roman Catholic herself, she also passed on her philosophy of television by giving regular lectures at the National Radio and Television Centre at Hatch End, the Roman Catholic training institution established by Father Agnellus Andrew OFM, formerly the Roman Catholic Assistant to the BBC's Head of Religious Broadcasting. She was 86 when she died at her flat in London.

15

Paul Fox

'Powers of persuasion'

Paul Leonard Fox, Kt 1991, CBE 1985, journalist, scriptwriter, born 27 October 1925, married 1948 Betty Nathan, two sons; BBC Television Newsreel 1950, Editor: Sportsview 1953, Panorama 1961, Head, Public Affairs Department 1963, Head, Current Affairs Group 1965, Controller, BBC1 1967–73; Yorkshire Television, director of programmes 1973–84, managing director 1977–88, chairman, ITV Network Programme Committee 1978–80; president, Royal Television Society 1985–92; chairman, Race Courses Association; Honorary LL.D. Leeds University 1984.

Paul Fox joined the BBC in 1950 by one of the most effective routes. He answered an advertisement for a holiday relief, and once inside he made good. During the Second World War he had been a big, burly member of the Parachute Regiment. He began his media career in 1946 as a reporter on the _Kentish Times_, and for the next three years he was a scriptwriter for Pathé News, as well as writing for _The People_. He had thoroughly mastered the art of matching words to moving pictures, and the temporary holiday relief job was similar, writing commentaries for the television newsreels which were produced at Alexandra Palace under the direction of Richard Cawston.

Paul Fox had entered a talented group. Other script-writers on the newsreel were David Wheeler, later Editor of *Panorama*, Stephen Hearst, an ex-trainee store detective at Marks and Spencer who was to become the Head of Arts Features and the Controller of Radio 3, and James Bredin, one of the founders of ITN and later managing director of Border Television.

Television Newsreel had originally been created by Philip Dorté who came from Gaumont-British. It was modelled on the type of newsreel shown in the cinemas, at first changed only once a week, later twice, and by 1950 with five separate editions weekly. It could not cover the up-to-the-minute news of the day because at that time the professional laboratories which developed and printed 35-millimetre film were not geared to the pace of daily news. Film sent to them for processing was not returned until the following day. And this was well before there were 16-millimetre sound film cameras of a professional quality, let alone video cameras.

Nevertheless it was a popular programme, and its coverage of the Korean war, with René Cutforth as reporter and Ronnie Noble as cameraman, was out-standing. The voice of *Television Newsreel* for over five years was Edward Halliday. During the Second World War he had worked with Sefton Delmer on black propa-ganda, subversive broadcasts in German purporting to originate inside Germany. He was also well known as a royal portrait painter. Those who had been watching television throughout the evening could catch up with the day's developments by listening to a recording of the most recent radio news bulletin which was transmitted against a clock modelled on Big Ben.

When Tahu Hole started his dreary version of television news (see Hole p. 130) many of the most able men on the old *Television Newsreel* had opted against joining this unattractive operation, Paul Fox persuaded Peter Dimmock, the Head of the Outside Broadcasts Department, to start *Sportsview* which quickly showed how live news, albeit restricted to sport, could be effectively presented. The *Sportsview* unit, run by Paul Fox and Ronnie Noble, firmly established the BBC's early lead in the coverage of sport, particularly its live handling of the Olympic Games at Rome in 1960.

After Hugh Carleton Greene was made Director of News and Current Affairs in 1958 Stuart Hood was moved to Alexandra Palace from Bush House to revitalise Tahu Hole's moribund television news operation. He made a good start at it, but fairly soon he was further promoted to become the television Programme Controller (see Dimmock, p. 165). Michael Peacock, the Editor of *Panorama*, and Paul Fox, the Editor of *Sportsview*, both applied for the Television News Editor vacancy. I expected Peacock to get it, because he had recently been commissioned, with two other high-powered television producers, to make a study of the television news operation and recommend ways of improvement. So I approached Paul Fox and said if Peacock was chosen (which in the event he was), would he be interested in taking over *Panorama*? Paul was very keen. He had been running sport for seven years and wanted to show that he had wider interests in the current affairs field.

One of the first of Fox's new tasks was to mount a special edition of *Panorama* from Moscow. The BBC had been involved in long negotiations to create the first live television link-up with the Soviet Union. It was technically difficult, and the Soviet jamming of BBC programmes in Russian was a political obstacle. The jamming was halted and the technical problems seemed solved when, early in 1961, Norman Collins, on behalf of Associated Television, proudly announced that they were going to achieve this first link-up bringing live coverage of the British Trade Exhibition in Moscow on 17 May.

Hugh Carleton Greene, by then the Director-General, was highly competitive by nature. After the BBC's long and difficult negotiations he was loath to let Collins get away with this scooping challenge. He told the television service to offer to relay the Moscow May Day parade live – more than a fortnight ahead of the British Trade Exhibition – saying that the Russians would be bound to agree, as indeed they did.

The Foreign and Commonwealth Office had great misgivings. They thought the BBC was offering the Russians a splendid opportunity to make propaganda for their cause. In the event it had the opposite effect. The sight of all that massive military hardware trundling across Red Square seriously undermined the picture of Russia as a peace-loving nation that was being fed to the Campaign for Nuclear Disarmament.

Because 1 May was on a Monday that year, it was decided also to have *Panorama* come from Moscow that night. Richard Dimbleby would present both programmes. Paul Fox went ahead to the Soviet Union to prepare the various ingredients of *Panorama*'s special edition. On 12 April he heard the news that the Russians had successfully launched the first man into space. Major Yuri Gagarin, 27 years old, had been sent up in a $4\frac{1}{2}$-ton Vostok spaceship. He had orbited the earth and was safely down after a flight lasting just under two hours. Paul used all his energetic driving force, with help from the other BBC men in Moscow, in a desperate attempt to get the link-up advanced by seventeen days so that we might relay Gagarin's triumphant home coming to Moscow Airport.

I was working late in my office at Lime Grove on 13 April when Paul Fox managed to get through on the telephone from Moscow to say they were now pretty certain they could get a circuit via Helsinki in time for the broadcast of Gagarin's arrival at Moscow Airport the very next morning.

I had no right to authorise a special transmission – there was no morning television in those days – but a quick decision was needed, so I arranged to tell the press and to start trailing immediately that we hoped to cover the reception of the first man to travel in space with the first live television pictures from Moscow. It could only be a hope because Paul had warned me that official Soviet permission had not yet come through and there was no chance of testing the circuit.

I corralled Richard Dimbleby and Anatol Goldberg from the BBC's Russian Service and at 10.30 on Friday, 14 April we opened transmission. We showed what little newsfilm had already come from Russia and Richard explained the complications of getting pictures along the route from Moscow over to Helsinki and then via the Eurovision network to London. He talked with Goldberg as we anxiously waited for pictures to come up on the studio monitor. At 10.46 a.m. miraculously they came through, and in good quality, though the sound was poor. But the sight of Major Gagarin walking alone across the vast tarmac of Moscow Airport to receive Khrushchev's bear-hug embrace needed no words of commentary.

A month later Major Gagarin paid an unexpected visit to London to appear at the Soviet exhibition at Earls Court. We were trying to mount a special edition of the programme *Press Conference* from the exhibition, at which the astronaut could be questioned by journalists. Fox handled the delicate negotiations with Comrade Rogov of the Soviet Embassy, who was worried lest secrets of the Soviet space programme should inadvertently be disclosed.

After a great deal of discussion it was agreed that Gagarin would take part, provided that one of the journalists on the panel was Yuri Fokin, a well-known Soviet broadcaster who was travelling with Gagarin, and that the general areas of questioning, though not the specific questions, would be submitted in writing in advance. Richard Dimbleby would be the chairman and the other journalist would be Tom Margerison, science editor of the *Sunday Times*. Boris Belitzky of Moscow Radio, whom Frank Gillard and I had got to know well on our Russian trip (see Gillard, p. 66), would be the interpreter.

The evening before the programme was due to be recorded Fox telephoned to say that, despite the earlier agreement, Rogov had been told to insist that every single question must be submitted in writing by 9.30 the next morning, otherwise the programme was off. I said that in that case the programme would have to be off, but I suggested that he should warn the Soviet officials that we would have to announce to the press why it was being cancelled. I urged him to go round to the Soviet Embassy the next morning to try to get them to return to the earlier agreement.

Paul has great powers of persuasion and he rang the next morning to say all was well. The Embassy had withdrawn its demand for written questions in advance. Gagarin, with Belitzky as interpreter, went to lunch with the Queen at Buckingham Palace and came straight on to Earls Court where we had set up our cameras.

The programme went smoothly. Gagarin answered the

questions easily and with great charm. At the end Dimbleby asked him what presents he was taking back to Moscow. There was a hurried consultation with Belitzky who then said, 'Major Gagarin is going to take back toys for his children, souvenirs of London, and something for his wife, which he will not disclose, in order that it may remain a surprise.' There were smiles all round.

After the programme Rogov said to Fox, 'Ah well, we all have to compromise.' Paul replied sharply, 'What do you mean? We didn't.' Later that day I said to Belitzky, 'There wasn't any serious risk to your security from the live questioning, was there?' He told me that the only embarrassing question had been the one about presents. The gift Gagarin had bought for his wife in London was a fur coat.

The next stage in Fox's upwardly mobile career came in 1963 when he was made Head of Public Affairs programmes. When the sudden news of President Kennedy's assassination came through, at about 7.30 in the evening of Friday, 22 November of that year, Paul Fox was one of the few senior television people on duty. Most of the others were at the annual awards dinner of the Guild of Television Producers and Directors, the predecessor of BAFTA. He immediately arranged to mount a special obituary programme later that night. Fox wanted to get tributes from the new Prime Minister, Sir Alec Douglas-Home, the Leader of the Opposition, Harold Wilson, and the Liberal leader, Jo Grimond.

The different activities those three leaders had chosen for the weekend provided a cartoonist's stereotype of the British political parties. The Conservative Prime Minister was on his way for a weekend's shooting with the Duke of Norfolk. There was no telephone in his car. (What price the four-minute warning for a nuclear attack?) But Fox managed to get an AA man to flag him down before he got to Arundel Castle, and give him the news. Sir Alec immediately returned to London, pausing only to exchange the bow tie he was wearing with his dinner jacket for a long black one. He went to Broadcasting House and was conducted to the small basement television studio by lift. The lift stuck, and he was released to speak the elegant words he had composed in the car only a matter of minutes before the programme began.

The Labour leader was addressing a political rally in North Wales. Wilson immediately agreed to take part, and the police led him on a fast drive to Manchester, the nearest injection place into the television network. But Manchester had no programmes scheduled for the weekend. The studios were locked, and Fox had great trouble getting hold of someone to open up and provide a crew to activate a studio.

Grimond, the Liberal, was making a speech at the Oxford Union. The officials there refused at first to interrupt the proceedings, until Fox made such a fuss on the telephone that they agreed to pass in a message. Grimond was happy to take part but had a logistical problem. The last train from Oxford to London had already left. No taxi or hire car was available. But two undergraduates offered to drive him to High Wycombe, where a BBC car would pick him up and take him to Lime Grove; they would climb into college afterwards. Grimond arrived after the programme had started, and used some of the same phrases as Douglas-Home, but no matter.

Meanwhile an ITV producer was trying to mount a similar emergency obituary programme and was somewhat miffed that Paul had already corralled all the main British political leaders. He suggested that these should also be made available to ITV and offered in return the

one senior politician he had managed to line up, George
Brown, who turned out to be rather drunk.

When Grace Wyndham Goldie finally retired in 1965,
Fox became Head of Current Affairs Group. He brought
Michael Charlton over from Australia to join the *Panorama*
team and started *24 Hours*. His colleagues greatly enjoyed
working with him. 'He makes everything he does seem
important,' one of them said.

In 1967 there was a shake-up in the structure of Inde-
pendent Television, with two new network companies,
Yorkshire Television and London Weekend Television,
being formed. Donald Baverstock, formerly the first Con-
troller of BBC1, was appointed Director of Programmes
at Yorkshire. Michael Peacock, the second Controller of
BBC1, became Managing Director of London Weekend.
Every Controller of BBC1, with the exceptions of Bill
Cotton and Alan Hart, has subsequently moved over to
ITV.

Paul Fox was Michael Peacock's successor as Controller
of BBC1, as he had been as Editor of *Panorama*. He was
an aggressive and successful scheduler and his channel
was held in high esteem between 1967 and 1973. I was at
that time in New York, which Paul visited regularly on
his way to search for good new American television series.
Satellite television across the Atlantic had just been established and we supplied his channel with much programme material on the Apollo space shots, political
assassinations, electoral developments and other topical
issues of that eventful period.

Running the New York office is one of the nicest jobs in
the BBC. Paul Fox used to tell me that it was the one he
would like to have next. But that was not to be. Ward
Thomas, the managing director of Yorkshire Television,

invited him in 1973 to be the Director of Programmes at Leeds, in succession to Donald Baverstock whose services were being dispensed with. It was far too good an offer to refuse, especially at a time when the BBC was complying with the government's request for a national wage freeze, and Paul badly needed a new car.

Under Fox's direction Yorkshire Television was soon established as a major contributor to ITV networked programmes. After two years he became managing director. He skilfully masterminded the company's flotation on the London Stock Exchange. He also played a leading role in the development of Independent Television News, as a director for nine years and as chairman for two. But he never severed his links with the BBC, and used regularly to contribute articles to *The Listener*.

At the end of 1987 the BBC television service was suddenly faced with a crisis. The Managing Director Bill Cotton would be 60, the BBC's normal retiring age, the following April. His departure had already been announced and he was looking forward to becoming an independent programme producer. His designated successor was the Director of Television Programmes, Michael Grade. But Grade had privately decided to apply for the vacancy as chief executive of Channel 4 rather than work under the new Deputy Director-General, John Birt, who had formerly been his underling at London Weekend Television. Grade was selected for Channel 4.

So both the top men at Television Centre would be leaving together. Although Paul Fox was already over 60 he was invited to return on a three-year contract to hold the fort as Managing Director. The television service was delighted to welcome him back and he provided the steadiness and the leadership that was called for.

Paul was knighted in the 1991 New Years Honours list.

He had previously received many other awards: the CBE, the Cyril Bennett Award of the Royal Television Society for his 'outstanding contribution to television programming', and a Fellowship of the British Academy of Film and Television Arts. For seven years he was the President of the Royal Television Society, succeeding Sir Huw Wheldon. He has for long been fascinated by horse racing, which he lists in *Who's Who*, with television, as his hobby. He was on his way to Ascot Races with one of his sons when he passed the fire raging at Windsor Castle and immediately stopped to telephone a vivid eyewitness account into the lunchtime television news.

He is now the chairman of the Race Courses Association, the trade association of fifty-nine race courses, and he serves on the committee concerned with the rewards and the responsibilities of the police. He continues to practise journalism, as he has done all his life. He would have made a great Fleet Street editor.

16

Peter Dimmock

'You've got to keep him.'

Peter Dimmock, CVO 1968, OBE 1961, born 6 December 1920, married 1960 Mary Freya (Polly) Elwes (died 1987), three daughters; 1990 Christabel Scott née Bagge; RAF pilot, instructor and Air Ministry Staff Officer 1939–45; journalist, Press Association; BBC Television Outside Broadcasts producer and commentator 1946, Assistant Head of Outside Broadcasts, Television, created Sportsview *Unit 1954, Head of Outside Broadcasts, Television 1954; sports adviser to European Broadcasting Union 1959–72; General Manager, Outside Broadcasts, BBC Television 1961, liaison executive between BBC and Royal Family 1963–77, General Manager, BBC Enterprises 1972–77; chairman, Sports Development Panel 1976–77; vice-president and managing director, ABC Worldwide Sales and Marketing, vice-president and subsequently consultant, ABC Video Enterprises Division, 1978–90.*

In the months before the launch of ITV in 1955 the new programme companies recruited many trained BBC television staff by paying them substantially higher salaries. The Director-General, Sir Ian Jacob, was normally reluctant to allow his television service to match these offers because of the inflationary effect on the BBC's grading structure. However, when Sir George Barnes, then Director of Television, rang the DG to tell him that an approach had been made to Peter Dimmock, Jacob said, 'Well, I don't mind what you do, but you've got to keep him. Make any sort of personal arrangements for him – as a personal case – that are necessary.'

Peter Dimmock was regarded as a personal case partly because of his skill in negotiating sports contracts, and in selling the programmes resulting from those contracts to broadcasting organisations abroad. From its earliest days, sport had been a keystone of the BBC's programme structure, and Dimmock had established excellent relations with all the sporting authorities. His unique knowledge of the BBC's sports contracts could have been invaluable to ITV, had it wanted to offer a first class sports service. In the event the early ITV companies were relatively uninterested in sport.

Moreover, Dimmock was also a particularly talented broadcaster. With his handsome features, sunny expression, well-trimmed moustache and clear voice he had been, since April 1954, the popular presenter of *Sportsview*, the first television sports magazine. Produced by Paul Fox, the *Sportsview* unit made full use of all the resources of the Outside Broadcasts Department, which Dimmock headed.

Sportsview was the first BBC programme to have a teleprompter. Dimmock, who had seen it being employed most effectively in the United States, realised its potential. He understood how to use it properly, keeping his face animated while he read, unlike many politicians and other would-be communicators at that time who tended to read off the teleprompter with a wooden expression. Earlier Dimmock had had experience as a jack-of-all-trades producer and commentator on racing and other outside broadcast events. Above all he had played a major part in organising the overall television coverage of Queen Elizabeth's Coronation on 2 June 1953 and had produced BBC television's most acclaimed programme, the Coronation Service from Westminster Abbey.

Cameras had been allowed inside the Abbey as a result of an intervention by the Queen herself. The Coronation Joint Executive Committee was the body ultimately responsible for the Coronation arrangements. It epitomised the Establishment, chaired by the Earl Marshal, the Duke of Norfolk, and including such VIPs as the Archbishop of Canterbury, the Queen's private secretary, the Commonwealth High Commissioners and, representing the Prime Minister, Jock Colville, private secretary to Sir Winston Churchill. This august group decided in the summer of 1952 that to have live television inside the Abbey during the Coronation would impose an intolerable emotional strain on the young Queen. The bright lights and their heat could easily prove to be a disastrously heavy burden on a long exhausting day. Moreover, it would deprive a then privileged class of peers and peeresses of the exclusive opportunity of witnessing at first hand the crowning of the new Queen.

The Cabinet, reviewing the Coronation arrangements on 10 July, agreed that no facilities should be provided for television inside the Abbey. It noted that a 'cinematograph film was to be taken, as in 1937', and considered that viewers' interests might be met if that film could be shown on television later in the day. As a reminder of the times, the Cabinet was informed, at its meeting a fortnight later, that each Briton's weekly meat ration would be raised from what one shilling and ninepence would buy to what two shillings would buy.

When Sir Winston conveyed to the Queen in October the unanimous view of her leading advisers, and of the Cabinet, that she should not be subjected to the ordeal of live television during the Coronation, she courteously reminded him that it was she who was being crowned, not the Cabinet, and that she felt all her subjects should have the opportunity of seeing it. Jock Colville disclosed in 1983, when the Coronation papers were made public under the 30-year rule, that as soon as Churchill returned from Buckingham Palace the Prime Minister told his private secretary the Queen's views and instructed him to summon a meeting to reverse the earlier decision to exclude live television. Thus the 26-year-old Sovereign personally routed the Earl Marshal, the Archbishop of Canterbury, Sir Winston Churchill and the Cabinet. They accepted the rebuff with good grace.

For a long time a legend persisted within the BBC that it was the Queen's grandmother, old Queen Mary, who tipped the scale in allowing television cameras into the Abbey, because she realised that she was too frail to be able to attend. In the event, she died before Coronation Day. Colville had been Princess Elizabeth's private secretary before serving Churchill in the same capacity. When I asked him about this he replied, 'I feel sure that the legend about Queen Mary and television is indeed only a legend. My mother was one of her Ladies in Waiting and indeed the closest to her, and with the Prime Minister's permission I used to go to see her every Thursday evening to tell her what was going on in the world. I am sure that if she had been keen on the Coronation being televised she would have told me. I rather doubt if she even had a set.'

In the meantime, Dimmock, the nominated producer, had been working hard to convince the Abbey authorities, with practical demonstrations, that the lighting level would not be oppressive and the cameras would not obtrude. It was decreed that the cameras must be at least 30 feet away from the Queen. Dimmock demonstrated the discreet long-distance picture that was obtainable with a 2-inch lens on the camera. On the day he used a 12-inch lens which showed the actual lowering of the crown in close-up. At the right moment he cued Richard Dimbleby, the commentator, to mention Prince Charles and cut to a charming picture of the 4-year-old prince in the royal box watching his mother being crowned.

The combination of Dimmock's impeccable camera direction and Dimbleby's felicitous words, together with the pageantry of the scene and above all the bearing of the young Queen, assured a television triumph. The viewing audience that day was over twenty million, many watching in friends' houses or in public places. It was for the first time larger than the radio audience, which was slightly under twelve million. Viewers in France, Belgium, the Netherlands and West Germany, able to see it through early Eurovision, were enraptured. The following year BBC television licences rose by 50 per cent. Television was set to become the nation's dominant medium of mass communication.

Dimmock was the son of a distinguished Marconi and later BBC engineer, and he always took a keen interest in television engineering developments, especially in America, which pioneered, for instance, the Image Orthicon Camera and the use of Ampex for immediate slow-motion replays. He fought vigorously for their adoption by the television service, sometimes against obstinate but understandable opposition from BBC engineering colleagues who felt that only equipment manufactured in

Britain should be used, even though inferior in performance.

Peter had been educated at Dulwich College, and when war broke out he joined the RAF. He served first as a pilot, later as a flying instructor, and finally as a staff officer at the Air Ministry. After the war he joined the Press Association as a journalist, and in 1946, like many former RAF pilots, he became a television producer and commentator in the Outside Broadcasts Department. He had been responsible for many of the major outside broadcasts, including the Olympic Games in 1948, the Boat Race in 1949, the first international relay from Calais in 1950, and the funeral of King George VI at Windsor in 1952. He was made Head of Television Outside Broadcasts in 1954.

Peter Dimmock wed the enchanting television announcer and *Tonight* reporter Polly Elwes in 1960. She had made her first television appearance on *Panorama* in an item dealing with people born on 29 February and thus only able to celebrate their real birthdays every four years. She was then engaged as a television announcer; in those days not just voice-over work, but what Eric Maschwitz called 'pulchritude in vision'. Polly came of a leading Roman Catholic family. Her father was a well-known judge. They were an attractive couple. Polly left announcing to become *Tonight*'s only female reporter. They had three daughters. Eventually she developed terminal cancer, against which she waged a long and brave fight until 1987.

In 1960, the year that Peter and Polly married, it was announced that Kenneth Adam, the Controller of Programmes, would shortly succeed the retiring Sir Gerald Beadle as Director of Television. Four people were invited to apply for the vacant programme controllership. They were Peter Dimmock, Hywel Davies, the head of programmes in Wales, Stuart Hood who was in charge of television news at Alexandra Palace, and myself. Hood was appointed, to the considerable surprise of the television service. He had done a good job over the two previous years in improving the somewhat moribund television news service. But prior to that he had been in the World Service at Bush House. He had had no experience whatever of television programme work.

There was no obvious successor at Alexandra Palace to take Hood's place as television news editor. Beadle had long cherished a hope of integrating news into the television service. Accordingly he proposed to Hugh Carleton Greene, the new Director-General who had been instrumental in selecting Hood, that news and current affairs for television should be combined and that I should be in charge of both, with deputies at Alexandra Palace and Lime Grove.

Carleton Greene turned down this suggestion, because it would break the unity of radio and television news, by which he set great store. However, as a gesture of confidence in the way we were handling current affairs, he wanted me to take the editorial responsibility not only for the output of the Television Talks Department, but also for other programmes involved with current affairs which were sometimes produced, for example, by the dramatised documentary section of Drama or by the Film Department. To signal this supervisory authority over programmes of other departments I was given the higher status of Assistant Controller, Current Affairs and Talks.

The vacancy for the editorship of television news was then advertised, and Michael Peacock, the whiz-kid Editor of *Panorama*, was selected. Meanwhile Beadle and Adam were having misgivings about Hood's appointment. They realised that many in the television service were feeling restive: the last two programme controllers had been appointed from outside its ranks. Was there never to be promotion from within the television service? Moreover Hood, with his soft voice and strong Scottish accent, was not very effective at communicating with the heads of his output departments, and he did not seem to appreciate the problems of making television programmes.

The retiring Director and his successor decided that Hood needed at his right hand an Assistant Controller who knew the television service inside out, and would prevent mistakes from being made. Of the unsuccessful candidates for the controllership, I had already been promoted; Davies was in line to be the next Controller, Wales. Sadly, he was to die before the vacancy occurred. That left Dimmock, and who was better qualified for the task than this thoroughly professional head of a main programme department, with his immense television experience both as a producer and as a performer?

Accordingly Beadle and Adam persuaded the Governors to create the new senior television post of Assistant Controller of Programmes. Unfortunately they failed to take the elementary precaution of checking with Dimmock beforehand whether he could accept it. When it was offered he turned it down, seeing no advantage in giving up the Outside Broadcasts Department and *Sportsview* merely to become Hood's minder.

No other departmental head was suitable, which left Beadle and Adam in an awkward quandary. They had convinced the Board of Governors that the new post was essential. Now they had no one to fill it. However, the whiz-kid from *Panorama* had been appointed Editor of Television News. Why not promote the other whiz-kid from Television Talks, Donald Baverstock, the Editor of

Tonight? Again they acted without consultation and quickly appointed him. Either of Baverstock's immediate bosses – my deputy, Grace Wyndham Goldie, or myself – would have told them that Donald Baverstock was a brilliant magazine editor but at that time had minimal experience of administration and of handling senior staff. His ill-considered over-promotion damaged both the television service and his own career.

By contrast Dimmock's career prospered. His title was changed to General Manager, Outside Broadcasts, giving him the status of an Assistant Controller, as well as various other perks. He also became the Sports Adviser to the European Broadcasting Union. He had been concerned on behalf of BBC Television with the EBU virtually from its inception in 1950, sport being one of the television programme areas in which language problems are minimal, and therefore particularly important for Eurovision.

From 1963 to 1977 Dimmock was responsible for liaison between the BBC and the Royal Family, a delicate task which he handled sensitively. An early embarrassing incident was not held against him. When the *Sportsview* unit was created in 1954 it regularly hired a commercial helicopter to ferry film quickly from Saturday football matches back to Lime Grove for use in *Sports Special*, the predecessor of *Match of the Day*. Dimmock was always keen to publicise the *Sportsview* unit, and arranged with the firm supplying the helicopter to have large placards marked 'BBC *Sportsview*' attached to its sides whenever his unit hired it.

In 1955 Princess Margaret and Group Captain Peter Townsend were invited by Lord Rupert Nevill to use the secluded garden of his house in Sussex one Sunday for a private discussion of their future plans. Following a tip-off, the *Daily Mirror* hastily hired a helicopter to swoop low over the garden so that they could be photographed (*plus ça change* . . .). Unfortunately it was the same machine as had been used the previous day for the football film, and the firm had failed to detach the 'BBC *Sportsview*' placards. The Director-General, Sir Ian Jacob, was immediately telephoned and given a rocket for the BBC's monstrous invasion of royal privacy. A Scotland Yard inspector rang Dimmock to ask what the hell *Sportsview* was doing. Eventually explanations were accepted and Dimmock was exonerated. It had all long been forgiven and forgotten by 1968 when the Queen made him a Commander of the Royal Victorian Order.

In 1972 the BBC decided to make use of Dimmock's entrepreneurial skills by appointing him General Manager of BBC Enterprises, the Corporation's selling arm. It badly needed better professional leadership, which he successfully gave. Five years later he might easily have been appointed managing director of Visnews, the international newsfilm agency, had not Sir Charles Curran, the retiring BBC Director-General, unexpectedly applied for the job. Instead Peter Dimmock accepted an offer from Roone Arledge, his opposite number in the American Broadcasting Company in New York, to become the vice-president of ABC Worldwide Sales and Marketing TV Sports. After several years in New York he was moved to Monaco as managing director of ABC Sports International, which was subsequently absorbed by ABC Video Enterprises.

For many years Peter seemed to shuttle between Monte Carlo and New York, dropping in from time to time to greet old friends at the Garrick Club. Three years after Polly's death he married Christabel, the widow of James Scott, and the eldest daughter of Sir John Bagge, Bt, a former High Sheriff of Norfolk. He is now partly retired, but still has a number of business interests concerned with television. His BBC achievements in broadcasting the ceremonial occasions of State and establishing pre-eminence in the coverage of sport will long be remembered.

17

Joanna Spicer

'The power behind the thrones'

*Joanna Ravenscroft Gibbon, CBE 1974, OBE 1957; born 29
April 1906, married Robert Spicer (died 1956), one son; Ministry of Information 1940; Empire Executive, BBC Overseas
Programme Administration 1941, Empire Service Programme
Planner 1943, Special Duties, Television Direction and Administration 1950, Television Programme Organiser 1952, Head
of Programme Planning 1955, Assistant Controller, Planning
1963, Assistant Controller, Television Development 1969;
retired from BBC 1973; consultant, Globo Television and International Institute of Communications; publication (with Asa
Briggs)* The Franchise Affair *1986; died 17 March 1992, aged
85.*

When George Campey, one of the early television correspondents, was stuck for a lead in his *Evening Standard*
column in the 1950s he was wont to type, 'What does
Miss Spicer think she is doing this time?' He would then
consult the *Radio Times* before castigating some aspect of
BBC television scheduling.

Joanna Spicer – she was Mrs, not Miss – was then
Television Programme Organiser and a leading executive
in the BBC, though virtually unknown to the general

public. She was the power behind the thrones of various Controllers of Programmes: Cecil McGivern, Kenneth Adam, Stuart Hood, Huw Wheldon and others, some of whom were inclined to accept more programme offers than they had either money or airtime for. She was the housekeeper who ensured that the Television Centre resources could meet the demands; or, rather, that we who were heads of programme departments cut our requirements to meet what was then a chronic shortage of studios, technical crews and film effort. We were all rather frightened of her.

Nowadays the complexity of matching programme planning to resources is facilitated by computers. In the 1950s, when nearly all programmes had to be transmitted live, and scheduling was infinitely more complicated, it was done by a tall, elegant, strong-willed lady with great charm and a first-class brain, supported by a small team of helpers who seemed to combine knitting with juggling coloured pieces of paper.

Another problem Joanna Spicer had to handle for the Programme Controller was compliance with the complicated government restrictions on the amount and kind of broadcasting allowed in the early days of television. In retrospect these shackles seem on a par with the need to have a man with a red flag walking in front of a Victorian motor car. The Post Office laid down the number of hours that could be broadcast each week. In addition there was an extra allowance for outside broadcasts of events not organised by the BBC, which was calculated on an annual rather than a weekly basis. There was a maximum limit on the percentage of American programmes in the schedule, and a similar minimum limit on the number of programmes of an educational nature. In planning the programme schedule Joanna had to take account of all these matters as well as the complicated television logistics.

Born Joanna Gibbon in 1906, she was educated at St Paul's Girls' School and Somerville College, Oxford. In the early part of the war she joined the Broadcasting Division of the Ministry of Information. She moved over to the BBC, by invitation, in 1941, and worked on the programme-planning side of the Overseas Service for nine years before transferring to television.

As BBC Television expanded, so did the complexity of its programme planning and its resources. Joanna Spicer was promoted to be Assistant Controller, Planning, and her last BBC post, to which she was appointed in 1969, was that of Assistant Controller, Television Development, responsible for advising the Managing Director of Television on the production resources that he needed, and on their best use.

There was at that time no post of Controller, Planning, or Controller, Television Development. The fact that Joanna Spicer was only given the title of Assistant Controller might be ascribed to a certain BBC male chauvinist swinishness in the 1960s. Perhaps it was a reaction from other powerful women such as Grace Wyndham Goldie in television and Mary Somerville in radio. A few days after Sir Ian Jacob retired, he was asked, on *Woman's Hour* of all places, which single word he would choose to characterise the BBC in his time as Director-General. Almost without hesitation he replied: 'Hagridden!'

David Attenborough has a different explanation. He notes that from its early days the BBC promoted women to high positions (see Russell, pp. 71–3). Huw Wheldon, who was the Managing Director at the time, maintained that the BBC's much-mocked system of titles was an expression of its priorities as well as its structure. The people at the top of television had all been programme makers. Joanna had not. It was imperative, Wheldon maintained, that programme people should be seen to hold the ultimate control of resources and cash. Therefore she could not be given the same titular rank as the Controllers of BBC1 and BBC2.

Attenborough adds that when he was Controller of BBC2 and making plans for colour transmissions, which started on that network in 1967, she suggested to him that BBC2 had the responsibility to show that this new technical development could truly enrich the cultural fare offered to viewers. It was that conversation which led to the first great success of BBC colour – Kenneth Clark's *Civilisation* (see Freeman, p. 231).

Joanna Spicer's second important task was to represent the programme side of BBC television at the European Broadcasting Union, and as such to be the focal point for Eurovision and satellite programme operations. She had a forceful voice in fluent French on the EBU Programme Committee. She was also effective in Italian. On one occasion she reprimanded a Venetian waiter so imperiously that he scurried away apologising, '*Si, Contessa, si Contessa.*'

ITV, who were relative newcomers to the Eurovision club, were anxious that Joanna should become their EBU representative, and dangled many attractive offers in front of her. But Sir Charles Curran, who was both Director-General and president of the EBU, kept extending her BBC contract, and she did not retire from the BBC until she was almost 67, well beyond the BBC's normal retiring age of 60.

For more than a third of her long life Joanna was a widow. Her much-loved husband Robert died suddenly in 1956. Cecil McGivern was then the Controller of

Programmes at BBC Television, and Joanna's immediate boss. He was a considerate and imaginative man. He immediately arranged for Joanna Spicer to go to the United States, where she had never been, to write a report for him on the current state of American television. Because I had recently spent ten years working in the United States he asked me to give her some introductions to people not professionally concerned with television.

I suggested she should visit friends of mine in New England, in the state of Washington on the west coast, and in Virginia. I must confess that I was rather apprehensive at the time. They might not be over-pleased at being asked to entertain a grief-stricken stranger. I should not have worried. Without exception they wrote letters back thanking me for sending such a delightful and charming person to see them.

Joanna Spicer was the first woman to be made a Fellow of the Royal Television Society. She was always a compulsive worker. Her husband's death had left her responsible for financing the education of their son through Eton and then Oxford. Even after retiring from the BBC she worked full-time as a consultant in the field of international communications, with a wide range of assignments in the United Kingdom and abroad, notably in Greece and Brazil. For ten years she was closely associated with Asa Briggs on the research programme of the International Institute of Communications, and they collaborated in writing *The Franchise Affair*, a study of the fortunes and failures of independent programme companies applying for television franchises in 1981.

Joanna Spicer managed to retain her slim good looks, her upright carriage and her zest for hard work even into her mid-eighties. She was then still writing a newsletter for the Friends of Unesco in Britain. She was one of the seminal but unknown influences in the growth of British and European television.

18

David Attenborough

*'An unspoilt person with an outsize
sense of fun'*

*David Frederick Attenborough, Kt 1985, CVO 1992, CBE
1974, FRS 1983, born 8 May 1926, married 1950 Jane Oriel,
one son one daughter; Royal Navy 1947–49; educational publishing 1949–52; trainee television talks producer, BBC 1952;
undertook zoological and ethnographic expeditions to: Sierra
Leone 1954, British Guiana 1955, Indonesia 1956, New Guinea
1957, Paraguay and Argentina 1958, south-west Pacific 1959,
Madagascar 1960, Northern Territory of Australia 1962, the
Zambezi 1964, Bali 1969, Central New Guinea 1971, Celebes,
Borneo, Peru and Colombia 1973, Mali, British Columbia, Iran,
Solomon Islands 1974, Nigeria 1975; Controller, BBC2 1965–
68, Director of Programmes, Television, and member of Board
of Management 1969–72, writer and presenter*: Tribal Eye
1976, Life on Earth 1979, The Living Planet 1984, The First
Eden 1987, Life in the Freezer 1993; *First Huw Wheldon
Memorial Lecturer, Royal Television Society 1987; pub-
lications*: Zoo Quest to Guiana 1956, Zoo Quest for a
Dragon 1957, Zoo Quest in Paraguay 1959, Quest in Para-
dise 1960, Zoo Quest to Madagascar 1961, Quest under
Capricorn 1963, The Tribal Eye 1976, Life on Earth 1979,
The Living Planet 1984, The First Eden 1987; *president,
British Association for the Advancement of Science 1992;*

Honorary Fellow, Clare College, Cambridge, Manchester Poly-
technic, UMIST; honorary degrees from Leicester, City,
London, Birmingham, Liverpool, Heriot-Watt, Sussex, Bath,
Ulster, Durham, Keele, Oxford, Bristol, Glasgow, Open Uni-
versity, Essex, Cambridge; Commander of Golden Ark
(Netherlands).

David Attenborough became a television star reluctantly,
helped by a timorous young chimpanzee. He had been
through the BBC's first television training course in 1952,
after a scholarship to Clare College, Cambridge, a degree
in zoology, national service in the Navy, and a brief spell
in publishing. He became a supernumerary young producer in the oddly named Television Talks Department,
mostly directing programmes which had been created by
other producers. A popular one at the time featured the
Superintendent of the London Zoo, George Cansdale,
who brought animals each week from the zoo to Alexandra Palace and demonstrated their peculiarities and
party tricks to viewers.

At the beginning of 1954, when I became Head of Television Talks, one of my first tasks was to battle for an extra
staff post to keep David Attenborough in the department.
Another was to secure enough foreign exchange, very
hard to come by in those days, to enable him to realise a
major programme proposal involving filming on location.

This was to mount – jointly with the London Zoo – an
animal-collecting expedition to Sierra Leone. Attenborough would direct a film record showing the Curator
of Reptiles, Jack Lester, searching for, and eventually cap-
turing, rare animals needed by the Zoo. Each film
sequence would end with a close-up of a captive creature
in Lester's hands. The programme would then mix to a

live studio situation where Lester, in the Cansdale manner, would demonstrate that particular animal's characteristics. There were to be six programmes altogether. The idea seemed promising and I backed it with most of the department's meagre allocation of foreign exchange.

Jack Lester was an excellent zoologist, but turned out to be a poor television presenter. The first programme of the *Zoo Quest* series was a near disaster. The technical complications of those days, when you had to move to an exact spot on the studio floor, look up at the correct one of four lenses on the television camera, and indeed at the right camera, and give a verbal cue precisely eight seconds before the next film sequence was needed, proved too much for him to master. He got everything wrong on the live transmission, and that also made him tongue-tied. After the programme the Controller of Programmes, Cecil McGivern, sent for me and declared in forthright terms that *Zoo Quest* had been a disgrace to the television screen. He was going to cancel the remaining five in the series. I pleaded with him for one more chance. Attenborough had brought back some splendid film material, I said, and we would retrieve the studio presentation somehow. 'You'd better,' McGivern warned me.

I told David: 'Jack Lester won't ever manage to remember the moves in the studio. You went on the expedition. You must go on to the studio floor and share the presentation with him. You give the film cues for telecine. You steer him to the right camera. I'll get someone else to direct in the gallery.' Attenborough was outraged. 'You can't do that to me,' he said. 'It's most unfair. You must let me be in charge in the gallery for my own first major series.' I said: 'David, this is an order.' He told me bluntly what he thought of me, and that he would only go on to the studio floor under protest. He was intent on being a producer, not a performer.

The next programme included a young chimpanzee named Jane, who was very frightened by the television lights and other paraphernalia. On transmission, as soon as she saw her familiar friend David, she clung round his neck and refused to budge throughout the programme. The sight of this sweet little frightened chimpanzee hugging her handsome young protector caused the whole television audience to 'ooh' and 'ah'. McGivern had no further need to worry.

For the next decade a *Zoo Quest* series became more or less an annual event, and David Attenborough recorded the adventures of making them in entertaining and bestselling books illustrated with photographs taken either by himself or by his enterprising film cameraman Charles Lagus. In 1955 *Zoo Quest* to Guyana, at that time British Guiana, ran into a lot of trouble. Lester fell ill with anaemia caused by a hookworm infection. Then he was thrown off a horse and broke two ribs. Attenborough himself had to take over the work of finding and catching the animals, although initially he lacked Lester's expert eye and trapping skill. From then onwards he led the expeditions himself, and greatly expanded his zoological expertise.

Attenborough and Lagus made ethnographic programmes as well as zoological ones. For instance, 1957 saw them in New Guinea, having first dived for a supply of goldlip pearl shells, which were a better form of currency than that provided by the BBC. They were then used to acquire birds of paradise.

Attenborough's letters to me gave a vivid picture of their progress. One said:

We managed, by good fortune, to film the entire ceremonial involved in buying a wife – the bridal price was twenty-four birds of paradise skins, six goldlip pearl shells, sundry cowries and two pigs. We encountered the party en route for the bride and I was hoping to film a savage dusky slinking coyly into the husky arms of her beplumed, painted, bearded suitor. Unfortunately she turned out to be a somewhat elderly lady with one son of two years and every sign that she might add to the score in the very near future. It didn't seem to me much of a bargain, bearing in mind the amount of pearl shell and paradise plumes.

Only a few days afterwards we became involved in a Kanama, a pre-courtship behaviour pattern (as I dare say Margaret Mead would phrase it) in which the youth of the village assemble in a low smoke-filled hut and sit in two concentric circles rubbing noses. Every time the mother superior sitting in the centre called, everyone changed partners. Charles and I, needless to say, were in there shooting, but all we got out of it were streaming eyes with the smoke fumes, and a bad infestation of fleas.

Because of the hazardous nature and uncertain duration of these trips it was difficult to schedule David's work in between *Zoo Quests*, and very often, after the end of a series, he was the only talks producer free to direct an unscheduled programme organised at short notice, such as a party political broadcast or an address to the nation by the new Prime Minister, Sir Anthony Eden, who, unlike his predecessor Sir Winston, relished appearing on television. Eden had a strong streak of vanity, and in order not to have to be seen putting on spectacles to read from notes or a teleprompter, he used to learn his television talks off by heart. David had many problems with him, which he handled with great tact.

In 1962 I left Television Talks to become executive secretary of the Television Extension Committee, which planned the start of BBC2. My successor and former deputy, Grace Wyndham Goldie, divided what by then had become a large programme output group into a number of different departments, headed by what she called her 'bright young men'. David Attenborough, who was by then one of the longest-serving talks producers, was not one of her favourites. By that time he had acquired a great reputation as a presenter of natural history programmes. He decided to resign from the staff and to concentrate on making expeditions to film wild life. He also wanted to improve his academic qualifications by working for a Ph.D. in social anthropology.

BBC2 was duly launched in April 1964, inauspiciously interrupted on its opening night by a massive power failure. The first Chief of BBC2, as the post was then called, was Michael Peacock, an ex-Editor of *Panorama*. Donald Baverstock, the begetter of *Tonight* who had unexpectedly been promoted to be Assistant Controller of Programmes, was made Chief of BBC1. Both reported to Stuart Hood, the relatively new Controller of Programmes. Only six weeks after the start of BBC2 Hood dropped a bombshell by announcing that he was leaving immediately to take up an appointment at Associated-Rediffusion as programme controller. He gave as his reason the better job security at the commercial company. A-R would allow him to work until he was 65, whereas the BBC's retirement age was 60. In fact, within a year A-R had dispensed with Hood's services.

BBC management was thrown into turmoil. It was essential to have a strong Controller of Programmes to arbitrate between the conflicting claims of Baverstock at BBC1 and Peacock at BBC2 for money and other television resources, never adequate for ambitious programme makers. It was particularly important to have someone who could dominate Baverstock, who had little talent for staff management, and had succeeded in putting up the backs of many of the departmental heads at Television Centre.

The obvious choice was Huw Wheldon, the Head of Documentary and Music Programmes. He, like Baverstock, was an exuberant Welshman. Moreover, he actually spoke Welsh, which Baverstock did not. During the hiatus following Hood's hurried departure both network chiefs had made claims to have their posts upgraded to controller status, and this had been agreed. Wheldon, who was senior in age and experience to both Baverstock and Peacock, was at that time technically their junior. When he was offered the Controllership of Programmes he made it a condition of his acceptance that the two of them must exchange jobs. Donald Baverstock, who was far less decisive than his public reputation portrayed, wavered for a long time. His demand for promotion to controller status had been conceded, but he convinced himself that he was being demoted and eventually he resigned.

Fortunately there was an excellent successor waiting in the wings. David Attenborough needed little persuasion to return to the BBC fold. His vitality and sunny personality immediately brought a new atmosphere to the television service and he rapidly improved the quality of the new channel. During the four years he was in charge of BBC2 he established major series such as Jacob Bronowski's *The Ascent of Man* and Kenneth Clark's *Civilisation*. It was Attenborough's use of the word 'civilisation' in connection with a series of colour films on art that persuaded Lord Clark to write and present the highly successful award-winning programmes (see Spicer, p. 174). Attenborough had fought strenuously for the introduction of colour to BBC2, and he achieved it in July 1967, with Wimbledon providing the first colour transmissions in Europe.

When Huw Wheldon was made Managing Director of BBC Television in 1969, David Attenborough became responsible for the programme output of both networks. He was given the title of Director of Programmes and a seat on the Board of Management. He was clearly being groomed for promotion to the Director-Generalship. BBC administration, however, was not really his forte, though he did it very well. In 1972, after eight years behind a desk, he again resigned to write and present major natural history programmes.

One was the thirteen-part series *Life on Earth*, which took three years to make, and involved him and the film crew in 1.5 million miles of travel. Two different hardback editions of the resultant book headed the bestseller lists for many weeks, and made him very well off. Other impressive series were *Tribal Eye*, *The Living Planet*, *Trials of Life* and *Life in the Freezer*, with its stunning pictures of Antarctica.

David Attenborough's entertaining natural history programmes combine meticulous scholarship with adventure and an enthusiasm to communicate. Just to watch him handling a wild creature tells one a great deal about both the animal and the man. These programmes have won for him every possible television award and – what is rare for a professional broadcaster – high academic distinction as well.

He was made a Fellow of the Royal Society in 1983 and knighted two years later. In 1992 he presided over the British Association for the Advancement of Science, and made his presidential address the occasion for a passionate defence of public service broadcasting and a troubled concern for its future. Seventeen universities have awarded him honorary degrees. The Queen has made him a Commander of the Royal Victorian Order in recognition of his skill in directing her Christmas Day messages over the years. Despite these honours he remains an unspoilt person with an outsize sense of fun.

19

Huw Wheldon

'The last of the great actor-managers
and the best Director-General the
BBC never had'

*Huw Pyrs Wheldon, Kt 1976, OBE 1952, MC 1944, born 7
May 1916, married 1956 Jacqueline Clarke (died 1993), one
son two daughters; Kent Education Committee staff 1939; com-
missioned Royal Welch Fusiliers 1940; served North Western
Europe and Middle East with 1st and 6th Airborne Divisions
(Major 1st Battalion Royal Ulster Rifles 1941–45); Arts
Council Director for Wales 1946; Festival of Britain Directorate
1949; BBC Television 1952–76: Publicity Officer 1952, Senior
Talks Producer 1954, Head of Documentary Programmes 1962,
Head of Documentary and Music Programmes 1963–65, Con-
troller of Programmes 1965–68, Managing Director 1969–75,
Deputy Director-General 1976; chairman, London School of
Economics 1975; president, Royal Television Society 1979; pub-
lications:* Monitor *1962,* Royal Heritage *(with J. H. Plumb)
1977; honorary degrees from Wales, Ulster, Oxford, Open University; Honorary Fellow, Manchester College of Art and
Design; died 14 March 1986, aged 69.*

Huw Wheldon joined the BBC Television service in 1952
as its Publicity Officer. He was a vivacious Welshman
with a beaky nose, a booming laugh and immense good
humour who had played a leading part in organising the

Festival of Britain, which had earned him the OBE. He was very good at handling the television correspondents. After the 1953 Coronation he gave out the audience reaction figures to the waiting press. A record figure, 98 per cent, had enjoyed it very much. The *Daily Express* correspondent asked what it was that the 2 per cent did not like. Paraphrasing Hilaire Belloc, Huw Wheldon immediately replied, 'Well, Bob, you must remember that if Our Lord came back to earth two per cent of the people would complain, "There He goes again, always walking on the water."'

In addition to being Publicity Officer, Huw presented *All Your Own*, a weekend teatime programme in which he interviewed talented boys and girls about their hobbies and their skills. He was never patronising when he talked to the children. He treated them sympathetically and with gusto. As a senior member of the television service he attended Programme Review, the weekly cabinet meeting of the heads of departments. He always made valuable contributions to our discussions and his views were widely respected.

In 1954 Andrew Miller-Jones, who held the post of senior producer in the Television Talks department, left the BBC for a year's research fellowship at Manchester University to study the psychological impact of visual stimuli. The vacant post, which was graded above that of the other producers, was advertised. That weekend Huw Wheldon telephoned. Could he come and see me at my home in Buckinghamshire? He had something he needed to discuss with me urgently. I wondered what kind of publicity crisis Television Talks had provoked.

Huw arrived and came straight to the point. Had he any chance of being appointed to the senior producer post? If so he would like to apply, although it would represent no promotion for him. I told him we should be delighted to have him in the department, but warned him that it might be a step downwards in his career. He would no longer be able to participate in the inner councils of the television service. Huw did not mind that at all. He said that the one thing he wanted to do was produce programmes. He had applied for the post of Publicity Officer somewhat reluctantly when his Festival of Britain job ended in order to get a foot in the BBC door.

An appointments board was duly held, and Huw Wheldon's quality of leadership, combined with his mature view of the nature and opportunities of television, outweighed the fact that he had no personal experience of directing programmes. The board had no hesitation in appointing him to the senior producer post.

We then had to arrange for Huw to learn the technique of television direction as quickly as possible, with the minimum loss of face. A nursery slope was *Facts and Figures*. This was a small programme designed to convey serious economic information. In Reithian terms it tried simultaneously to combine information, education and entertainment. Frank Blackaby, the distinguished economist, provided the statistics. I narrated the programme. The entire visual content, which made the programme entertaining, was created by Alfred Wurmser. He was a Viennese designer who used to make ingenious and amusing graphic effects out of cardboard and string, with paper fasteners and pieces of wood. They produced fascinating pictures which moved in real time, unlike the laborious animations of the film industry. This was well before the development of electronic graphics, which revolutionised the whole animation process.

Facts and Figures communicated ideas through the eye

and the ear simultaneously in a form that was peculiar to television and was in no way derived from radio, the stage, the platform or the press. The rehearsal sessions of *Facts and Figures* were particularly useful to directors under training because they emphasised the importance of co-ordinating picture and sound. Moreover, the professionalism of Wurmser and his team would never let a trainee down. In the course of time Huw Wheldon took over the narration himself.

He also learned to produce *Press Conference*, a programme with four journalists interviewing someone in the news; it was simple enough to direct but often involved delicate negotiations with the guest interviewee, especially if he was as big, in all senses of the word, and as unpredictable as Orson Welles. Welles rapidly became a friend of Wheldon, and indeed later tried to enlist him as his European manager. Together they mounted *Orson Welles' Sketchbook*, a series which allowed Welles to reminisce in a highly entertaining fashion.

General Sir Brian Horrocks, then Black Rod, had been the Commander of XXX Corps at Arnhem. He wrote one day to his fellow general Sir Ian Jacob suggesting that he might give a series of television talks on battles in which he had been involved in the Second World War. Jacob sent the correspondence to Cecil McGivern, the Controller of Programmes, with a note saying that 'Jorrocks' was one of the best communicators among the military leaders.

McGivern clearly had to see Horrocks, and asked me to join him at a meeting in his Television Centre office early one morning. He said to me beforehand, 'I can't think of a television programme more offputting than a general rehashing the details of his battles in the last war. But of course we will listen to him courteously, and then I shall look at my schedules for the next quarter, and will explain that they are full up, but that we will bear the idea in mind for possible use in the future.'

Horrocks duly arrived. Leaning forward in his chair he began to tell us exactly what it felt like to be the general in command on the eve of an important battle, what sort of things would go through his mind. His description was so riveting that McGivern was soon reaching for his schedules to see where something could be dropped to make a suitable space for a Horrocks series.

My task was to allocate a suitable producer. Despite Huw's limited experience in the production gallery there could be no other choice. He had a fine military record. He was commissioned into the Royal Welch Fusiliers in 1940 and later transferred to the Royal Ulster Rifles because it had vacancies in a battalion earmarked for airborne forces. They landed by glider in Normandy on the evening of D-Day a few miles inland from 'Sword' Beach and their task was to secure bridges and high ground at the eastern edge of the Allied landings by sea. Major Wheldon received the Military Cross, in the field, from Field-Marshal Montgomery, for bravery under fire.

Wheldon immediately hit it off with Horrocks. He refused to let the general's delivery be deadened by the use of a teleprompter. Horrocks used to walk around Hyde Park learning his script off by heart. When he addressed the camera, live, his whole personality seemed to burst through the screen. *Men in Battle*, which began in March 1956, was an instantaneous success.

A week after Harold Macmillan became Prime Minister in 1957 Huw produced his broadcast from 10 Downing Street, which took the form of a fireside chat using a teleprompter. In a prescient report to me afterwards he wrote,

Teleprompters are a dangerous friend. They undoubtedly work, but the time will come when the present Prime Minister or others will want to come to the country as 'Mr Sincerity'. They won't be able to do without their teleprompters, and in a very real sense the use of this equipment will invalidate an approach of this sort.

Wheldon enjoyed appearing in front of the cameras himself, and he was sometimes used as an interviewer on *Panorama*. We were mesmerised by his flamboyant confrontation with Mike Todd, the film producer and third husband of Elizabeth Taylor. One television critic described it as like watching someone who had taken three benzedrine tablets interview someone who had taken five.

In November 1956, when he was 40, Huw married Jacqueline Clarke, usually known as Jay, who was then working with Dr Hilde Himmelweit and others on an empirical study of the effect of television on the young. Jay and Huw had a son and two daughters. She was a very talented novelist who had the misfortune to go seriously deaf in later life. She died in 1993.

In the 1950s we revived the *Brains Trust* on television on Sunday afternoon and radio carried the soundtrack the following Tuesday. It suited our colleagues in radio, who got the programme more cheaply that way than by mounting it themselves. In the course of time there was very strong pressure on us from Broadcasting House to adopt a similar arrangement for *The Critics*, the long-running programme on which an erudite panel discussed current films, plays, art exhibitions and so on. We resisted this proposal. It was all right, we argued, for a television programme that discussed ideas to consist merely of talking heads, but a programme involving the arts, and particularly the visual arts, must be conceived in visual terms. This was the origin of *Monitor*.

We were also anxious to find some suitable programme for Huw to present. With Celtic eloquence and an extrovert personality he was a very good performer on the screen. Traditional BBC practice then frowned on the use of staff as leading characters in current affairs magazines but there was no such inhibition regarding arts programmes. Having been the Welsh Director of the Arts Council, and then in charge of all Arts Council activities in connection with the Festival of Britain (including arranging 280 concerts), Huw was well equipped to play such a role.

There was a slight hiccup while the relative responsibilities of the producer and the editor/presenter of *Monitor* were sorted out. A number of talented film directors were assembled, some of them recruited from *Tonight*. They included John Schlesinger and Ken Russell, and their work was assembled by one of the best film editors in the business, Allan Tyrer. Humphrey Burton, David Jones and Melvyn Bragg were also part of the *Monitor* team built by Huw.

Monitor, which was launched on 2 February 1958, and *Face to Face*, which started a year later, alternated on Sunday evenings. Between them they brought a new audience to BBC television, finally breaking the resistance of the hard core of intellectuals who tended at that time to equate watching television with playing on machines in an amusement arcade. Huw showed the work and, in skilful interviews, revealed the inspiration of a wide range of artists, musicians, sculptors, poets and people of the theatre.

One one memorable occasion Huw felt that a complete edition of *Monitor*, as it had been prepared by the team, was below standard. It could have been transmitted, but it should have been much better. So he ordered the programme to be scrapped and completely remade overnight. Everyone had to work through the night. Sandwiches and hot coffee were laid on. Scripts were retyped. The Mark II *Monitor* was finished in time, and was hailed as a great success. Moreover, an important lesson was learnt.

Huw's career in the television service made steady progress, not only as a producer and a performer, but particularly as a leader. He became Head of Documentary Programmes in 1962, with responsibility for music programmes added the following year, and in 1965, after a spectacular leapfrog, Controller of Programmes (see Attenborough, p. 185).

The next three years saw many new programmes that provided delight or insight, Huw's personal criteria for television excellence. They ranged from *The Wars of the Roses* to *Till Death Us Do Part*, from *Dad's Army* to *Cathy Come Home*. He knew when to praise and when to blame. Above all, he knew when to delegate. That period also saw the introduction of colour television.

David Attenborough, always a close friend of Huw, described him as the last of the great actor-managers and the best Director-General the BBC never had. All of us fully expected Wheldon to become DG when Sir Hugh Greene's term ended. But that was before Harold Wilson's surprising appointment of Lord Hill of Luton to move overnight in 1967 from the chairmanship of the Independent Television Authority to that of the BBC.

Lord Hill appears to have come to Broadcasting House with two aims in mind. One was to get rid of Greene in an orderly fashion as soon as the right opportunity presented itself. The other was to ensure for himself a position of absolute power, altering permanently the traditional relationship between the full-time professional Director-General and the part-time amateur Chairman. He, not the DG, was to be Mr BBC.

The first objective was achieved more easily than he expected. In 1968 Greene was about to be involved in a second divorce, and failure to reach a satisfactory financial settlement was forcing him to contest the action his wife was bringing. This would mean that full details of Greene's murky private life were likely to be spread over the pages of the *News of the World* and other tabloids. He had to warn Hill of this possibility and offer to retire. In the event an agreement over money was reached, and the divorce proceeded without the publicity attendant on a contested action. Hill's only problem was to convince a sceptical public that he had not personally been the hatchet man behind the early retirement (see Greene, p. 109).

Greene's principal lieutenants, the Directors of Radio and Television, Frank Gillard and Kenneth Adam, were both nearing retirement age. Oliver Whitley, his Chief Assistant, had only three years left. Thus the leading candidates for the succession were Huw Wheldon and the Director of External Broadcasting, Charles Curran, who until recently had been the BBC's Secretary. The Secretary, who is present at every Board meeting, tends to be better known to the Governors than anyone else on the BBC staff, with the exception of the Director-General himself. Lord Hill in his memoirs recorded that no Governor showed any enthusiasm for Huw Wheldon as Director-General except, he claimed unconvincingly, himself. Hill also declared, with obvious satisfaction, that 'One governor said that a less well-known Director-

General might be an advantage now that we had a strong Chairman.'

Hill never had any intention of sharing the limelight. The choice of Curran, who was virtually unknown to the general public, assured this. Moreover, Curran was the first Director-General to be appointed by a Chairman who had had at least as much broadcasting experience as he had, if not more. It was a move that greatly enhanced the power of the BBC Chairman at the expense of that of the DG (see Hill, p. 263).

Wheldon's consolation prize was promotion the following year to become Managing Director of Television. He was the first to hold that title, which gave him the ultimate responsibility for both money and programmes. This change implemented a recommendation from McKinseys, the management consultants whom Hill had engaged. It was the first, but not the last, time that outside managerial advice was sought. McKinseys' plan to pass the control of all BBC money to the budgets of the Managing Directors of Radio, Television and the External Services further diminished the role of the Director-General. Curran had to go cap in hand to the Managing Directors to ask for money to get the Governors' dining-room redecorated.

Huw Wheldon articulated the merits of public service television with a powerful voice, both at home and abroad. He frequently took the battle into his opponents' territory, as, for instance, when he spoke in 1971 to an audience consisting largely of architects. The BBC had recently been belaboured by the Campaign for Better Broadcasting, many of whose protagonists were architects. Huw began his address by musing aloud whether the broadcasters should start a Campaign for Better Architecture. He recalled the great curse in Samuel Beckett's play, *Waiting for Godot*, which finished with the three insulting words: 'imbecile, cretin, critic', and he went on to remind his audience that the original version was written in French and read: *'imbécile, crétin, architecte'*.

After that opening volley Huw went on to analyse what was required to make good programmes which were also popular:

'It needs an organisation which can provide a climate of work in which both programmes and the whole process of making them on the one hand, and the public on the other, are taken very seriously indeed. It also calls for producers and directors who, among their other qualities, have a certain generosity: who will above all work for the sake and for the good of the writers and the performers of the story or subject or theme which they are serving, and not for their own greater glory.'

To nurture and cherish writers was always part of the Wheldon creed. He felt strongly, and would make the point emphatically, when talking to American television moguls, that programmes like *Dad's Army* and *Till Death Us Do Part* had to be crafted by writers with inspiration, and could not become formulas to be extended by a script team into thirty-nine episodes. A programme must be rested when its originator's creative energy began to flag, regardless of its current place in the audience ratings.

He made several trips to the United States while he was Managing Director of Television. One coincided with a party being given in New York by ZDF, the second German television network, to welcome a new television correspondent. It was a buffet supper with small tables, and Huw and I found ourselves sitting with Chet Huntley, one of the leading newscasters of the National Broadcasting Company, and the new German correspondent. Sensing he had the ear of the Anglo-American media, the

German opened the conversation by saying, 'I am very worried about the image of West Germany in both America and Britain. What do you think we ought to be doing to improve our image?' Former Major H. P. Wheldon MC slapped his thigh, gave one of his booming laughs, and said, 'It's not your image, old boy, it's your reputation!'

Huw was saddened by the departure of his deputy, David Attenborough, at the end of 1972, to resume making major natural history programmes, and by that of Paul Fox shortly afterwards to move to Yorkshire Television. He himself was asked to leave Television Centre five months before his sixtieth birthday. This was to enable Ian Trethowan, then Managing Director of Radio, who was being groomed by Hill for the Director-Generalship, to have experience of running the television service. As a sweetener Wheldon was given a further year's employment on full salary as an adviser to Charles Curran with the courtesy title of Deputy Director-General. His main task was to write a report on the regions. He was knighted in the 1976 New Year Honours list.

Huw had also begun to do other things. He became chairman of the Court of Governors of the London School of Economics, his alma mater, and in 1977 he presented a major series of documentary programmes, *Royal Heritage*. This project was produced by Michael Gill, who had also made Kenneth Clark's *Civilisation* and Alistair Cooke's *America*. It dealt both with the royal collections and with the role of kingship in British history. Many of the Royal Family took part. The Queen described the State crown and the Queen Mother gave a conducted tour of her gardens at the Castle of Mey. The Duke of Edinburgh was seen driving a four in hand, and Prince Charles rowing on a loch.

Sir John Plumb, later the Master of Christ's College, Cambridge, was the historian who wrote the text from which the scripts were produced. Huw Wheldon was the presenter and, in a sense, the populariser. As is customary with major series of this sort, the programmes yielded a lucrative book.

For a while *Royal Heritage* had been in jeopardy. In the middle of the filming Huw had to undergo an operation for cancer. It would have been impossible to substitute another anchorman. Fortunately he recovered and his own performances in the series were some of the best he ever gave. There was one particularly memorable shot which showed a youth cleaning the crystals of one of the massive chandeliers in the Waterloo Chamber at Windsor Castle, while Huw, watching with his head on one side, pointed out that the chandelier weighed more than the boy.

Royal Heritage earned him the Silver Medal of the Royal Television Society, of which he became president in 1979. His last years were busy ones. He collaborated well with Ralf Dahrendorf, the director of the London School of Economics. He and Lady Wheldon regularly attended the Institute for Humanistic Studies at Aspen, Colorado, where he conducted seminars. He acted as an adviser to the National Broadcasting Company. He gave one of the Dimbleby lectures, after rehearsing it twice in front of his tolerant friend Sir Denis Forman, the chairman of Granada Television. Paul Ferris who wrote a posthumous biography of Huw Wheldon called it *Sir Huge*, an appellation actually used of Hugh Greene. Sir Denis's review of the book, which dismissed it as being 'wholly unworthy of its subject', was a judgement shared by all who had worked closely with him.

Sir Huw enhanced the reputation of the Royal

Television Society during the years of his presidency, and after he died the Society established an annual Huw Wheldon Memorial Lecture, the first of which was given at the National Museum of Film, Television and Photography in Bradford, appropriately by Sir David Attenborough. The RTS also gave Sir Huw a farewell dinner on 10 December 1985. He was in sparkling form, though it was only three months before his death from a resurgence of cancer. After listening to elegantly worded encomia from Stuart Sansom, Phil Sidey, Paul Fox and Bill Cotton, Huw quoted a remark of President L. B. Johnson, 'I wish that my parents could have lived to hear those words. My mother would have loved them, and my father would have believed them!'

20
Cliff Michelmore

*'An ability to rescue the programme
from any kind of crisis'*

*Clifford Arthur Michelmore, CBE 1969; born 11 December
1919; married 1950 Jean Metcalfe, one son one daughter; RAF
(Squadron Leader) 1935–47; Head, Outside Broadcasts and
Variety, British Forces Network (BFN) 1948; Deputy Station
Director BFN, also freelance commentator and producer,
Hamburg 1949, and BBC 1950; producer* All Your Own;
presenter: Highlight *1955–57*, Tonight *1957–65*, 24 Hours
*1965–68; General Election results programmes 1964, 1966,
1970,* So You Think ... *from 1966,* Our World *1967,* With
Michelmore *(interviews),* Talkback, *Apollo space pro-
grammes 1960–70,* Holiday *1969–86,* Chance to Meet *1970–
73,* Wheelbase *1972,* Getaway *1975,* Globetrotter *1975,*
Opinions Unlimited *1977–79,* Day by Day *(Southern
Television) 1980,* Sudden Change *(HTV) 1982,* Cliff
Michelmore Show *(BBC Radio) 1982–83,* Home on Sunday
(BBC TV) from 1983, Waterlines *(BBC Radio) from 1984,*
Lifeline *(BBC TV) from 1986; Television Society Silver Medal
1957, Guild of TV Producers Award, Personality of the Year
1958, TV Review Critics Award 1959, Variety Club Award
1961; publications: (ed.)* The Business Man's Book of Golf
1981, Cliff Michelmore's Holidays by Rail *1986, (with Jean
Metcalfe)* Two-way Story *1986.*

After the war in Europe had ended BBC Radio regularly broadcast *Two-Way Family Favourites* on the Light Programme. It was produced jointly from London and from the British Forces Network in Hamburg to a Sunday lunchtime audience of some twelve million.

Jean Metcalfe, the London presenter, had been a secretary in the Overseas Service when Haley's General Forces Programme for the troops worldwide started in 1944 (see Haley, pp. 83–4). They wanted announcers who sounded like the girl next door, and invited Jean to become one of them. She played record requests in *Family Favourites*, which became *Two-way Family Favourites* after the British Forces had set up their own radio station in Hamburg. Squadron Leader Clifford Michelmore – he had joined the RAF before he was 16 and was commissioned in 1940 – was at that time the Deputy Station Director of the British Forces Network. He had covered everything from boxing bouts to gardening talks and been responsible for outside broadcasts and variety. In an emergency, when the sergeant who had been the regular presenter of *Two Way Family Favourites* fell ill, Cliff Michelmore took his place.

Without meeting Jean Metcalfe except over the airwaves – or to be precise, over a disused underground military telephone line – Cliff gradually fell in love with her voice and personality. Eventually they did meet, in the Light Programme continuity suite in Broadcasting House. 'You must be Jean.' 'You must be Cliff.' They were soon married.

Jean's career in radio blossomed. In addition to announcing, she became an outside broadcast commentator at ceremonial events such as the Coronation and the Queen's visit to Northern Ireland. She was also one of the comperes, as they were then called, of *Woman's Hour*.

In 1955 she won the *Daily Mail* Radio Personality of the Year award. Her immediate predecessors were Richard Dimbleby and Gilbert Harding.

Cliff resigned from the RAF and the British Forces Network and began a freelance career at the BBC, working as a sports commentator in both radio and television. He soon moved into the production of children's television programmes, notably *All Your Own*, introduced by Huw Wheldon (see Wheldon, p. 190). It showed children enjoying their hobbies and displaying their talents. He also took part in many programmes for the West Region.

As the start of commercial television drew near both Jean and Cliff were approached with lucrative offers to move over to the other side. The BBC countered with inducements to remain. Jean was upgraded and given more interesting work. Cliff, still a freelance, was guaranteed a substantial annual income in fees. He acted as a reporter on *Saturday Sport*, he did several stories for *Panorama* in addition to producing children's television.

At that time, when evening television only began at 7.30 p.m., the Post Office set a strict limit on the number of hours of television that the BBC might transmit each week. However, when ITV started in 1955 the Post Office allowed the evening's viewing to begin at 7 p.m.

Unfortunately this daily increase of thirty minutes' television time was not accompanied by any more studio space or film resources, which were then what limited programme expansion. Every production studio at Lime Grove was fully committed, so Cecil McGivern, BBC Television's Controller, decided to fill the extra time with a quarter of an hour of news originated from a studio at Alexandra Palace, followed by a daily television version of *The Archers* produced in Birmingham.

The pilot programmes of *The Archers* were not up to standard, and at short notice McGivern asked if the Television Talks department could provide a substitute daily programme. He warned me that it would have to be mounted, alongside the weather forecast, from the tiny Lime Grove presentation studio. There would be no opportunity for studio rehearsal, and no film resources were available.

These restrictions did not worry me. A few months earlier, at the end of March 1955, no national newspapers had appeared for four weeks because of a strike of electricians and maintenance engineers. I had suggested then to McGivern that we should mount a daily programme with a panel of journalists reporting on and discussing the news they would have written for their newspapers. It was produced virtually without rehearsal, which proved it could be done.

That was the origin of *Highlight*. I asked Grace Wyndham Goldie, on her return from compassionate leave after the death of her husband, to supervise the programme in detail. It was produced brilliantly by Donald Baverstock, assisted by Alasdair Milne and Cynthia Judah, with virtually no resources and not much programme allowance, but with plenty of bright ideas.

The Archers may have muffed their own television launch, but with panache they pre-empted the press coverage of ITV's Guildhall launch by having Grace Archer (played by Ysanne Churchman) die in a brave attempt to save a horse from a blazing barn. Baverstock immediately invited *The Archers'* writers to be interviewed on *Highlight* by its initial presenter, MacDonald Hastings, father of the *Daily Telegraph's* Max Hastings. Mac introduced the item with the words 'And now for a slight case of murder.' Castigated for causing national grief, the scriptwriter Ted Mason countered by demanding, 'Why blame us? Did people blame Shakespeare for the death of Desdemona?'

McGivern considered Hastings the wrong choice for anchorman, and he was quickly replaced by two former television producers who took fortnightly turns to present *Highlight*. One was the sandy-haired Geoffrey Johnson Smith, whom I had first met in Washington when he and Robin Day were on an Oxford Union debating tour, and who was later to become a Conservative MP. The other was Cliff Michelmore, large, relaxed, with an infectious grin and an ability to extricate the programme from any kind of crisis.

Highlight usually consisted of three interviews, some serious, some light-hearted, often down the line to a regional studio. Cliff had a testing time during his first trial week as presenter. The contents one evening were due to be a discussion with a financial journalist on the state of the economy, an interview over the circuit to Cardiff with a Welsh author about a new production of *Under Milk Wood* and finally a short talk with a young Scot who had just won the World Ham Slicing Championship.

The financial journalist's underground train broke down at Notting Hill Gate, and he failed to arrive. The lines between Lime Grove and Cardiff collapsed and the Welshman could not be heard. Cliff had to make the discussion of the finer points of ham slicing last for twelve minutes instead of two. It in no way fazed him. He kept the programme both going and interesting, and finally was sent home rewarded with quantities of the property ham that they had had to keep slicing in the studio.

The *Highlight* production team took endless trouble to establish a style of questioning that was finely honed and precise. Most interview programmes at that time, especially on radio, tended to be obsequiously soft. *Highlight*'s questioning had edge. The programme soon acquired both authority and a large loyal following.

After eighteen months the limited facilities of *Highlight* made Baverstock and Milne restive. They badly wanted to create a more ambitious programme. After strong pressure from ITV the Post Office again allowed an increase in viewing hours, this time closing the gap between 6 and 7 p.m. McGivern was uncharacteristically indecisive about how best to fill what was known as the 'Toddlers' Truce'. Eventually he told me that he intended to start with a news summary. Then he wanted Television Talks to provide a weekly scientific programme. The Drama, Light Entertainment and Regional programme departments would contribute narrative programmes on the other nights.

We managed to persuade him that filling the early evening with a daily topical magazine based on the established success of *Highlight* would be much better suited to the needs of a changing audience at that time of day. A major problem with any new magazine programme is the right name for it. There is a limited number of suitable generic titles. *Man Alive* was considered and rejected, to be taken up later by Desmond Wilcox. George Campey, then BBC Television's Press Officer, who could seldom resist a pun, suggested *High Tea Vee*. The production team finally opted for *Tonight*.

At that time the National Broadcasting Company in the United States had a daily programme, generally known as the Jack Paar Show, later to become the Johnny Carson Show, but its proper title was *Tonight*. It was an evening chat show, hosted by a stand-up comic, and totally different from the programme we were planning. But I thought it would be courteous to assure Julian Goodman, the president of NBC News, that though we were calling our programme *Tonight*, it was in no way a copy of the Jack Paar Show. I had no reply from him, but NBC's lawyers told us it would be all right for the BBC to use their title *Tonight* provided we paid them 10 dollars every time the programme went out. I noted that NBC were then carrying a regular programme called *Home*. I got the BBC New York office to tell the NBC lawyers that BBC Television had a regular programme called *Home* on the air in 1937 and suggest that they should pay us retrospectively for their use of our title. That ended the matter.

Tonight began on 18 February 1957, running from 6.05 to 6.45 from Monday to Friday, with the jazz programme *Six Five Special* filling the space on Saturday. Cliff was the anchorman of the programme, assisted by Geoffrey Johnson Smith and joined by Derek Hart, the sardonic actor who had played Bob Dale in *Mrs Dale's Diary* for a couple of years. The programme often managed to include pungent comment in the form of calypsos sung by Cy Grant or Rex Harrison's son Noel. *Tonight* rapidly became compulsive viewing for large audiences. Because it aimed at being topical there was little time for detailed rehearsals. This was where Cliff Michelmore's long experience in broadcasting and unflappable temperament were invaluable. When things went wrong in the studio, as they often did, he would give a graceful and usually rather amusing apology. Because he was obviously not discomfited neither were the viewers.

The success of *Tonight* was due to a number of factors. It was brilliantly edited by Donald Baverstock, supported by a very strong team. It had some excellent film reports, especially from Slim Hewitt, the lugubrious-looking cameraman-turned-reporter who had been recruited from the dying *Picture Post*, which supplied many of *Tonight's* staff. It had a catchy signature tune, 'Tonight and Every Night'. Above all, it signalled the end of mandarin broadcasting. It spoke for its audience rather than to its audience. As the *Sheffield Star* put it, 'The success of *Tonight* is that it belongs to us.' Cliff Michelmore's contribution was marked by the award of the Television Society's Silver Medal in 1957 and his selection in 1958 by the Guild of Television Producers (the predecessor of BAFTA) as the Television Personality of the Year.

Tonight was steadily pulling in an audience of some eight million people and Cecil McGivern wanted us to keep it going all the year round, like the news. It was necessary to remind him that a team like *Tonight*'s had to have a proper break in order to recharge the creative batteries. It was no good trying to keep it going with a second eleven. Moreover, the strain on Cliff Michelmore of appearing friendly and affable on the screen five nights a week was such that a decent yearly holiday was essential. Under different editors Michelmore introduced *Tonight* for eight years and *24 Hours* for a further three.

Cliff was by this time busily involved in all major current affairs programmes which required an outstanding anchorman, General Election results, Apollo space programmes, the obituary tribute to Robert Kennedy and countless others. One of the most ambitious of these was *Our World*, a live global hookup beginning at 8 p.m. on Sunday, 25 June 1967, British time. The programme involved four satellite systems and more than a million miles of communication by telephone. The technical complexities of such a large-scale live operation needed someone of Cliff's experience and temperament to hold it together. It was the first worldwide television programme combining live messages and pictures from around the world beamed up to and down from a mirror in the sky.

Our World was supposed to concentrate on what unites the human family rather than the violent actions that divide it, and all had agreed that no politicians or heads of state would be included. Eighteen countries took part. There should have been five more but a few days before transmission the countries of the Soviet bloc pulled out in protest against Israel's Six-Day War earlier in the month.

Gradually Cliff Michelmore has moved towards more relaxing programmes, particularly those concerned with his own favourite leisure pursuits, sailing and holidays. He has also broadcast many programmes for Independent Television. He has always had a strong religious faith and is frequently seen in what is irreverently called the 'Godslot' – the programmes placed on Sunday evening at the time of Evensong. Cliff Michelmore is particularly gratified that his son Guy, like Richard Dimbleby's boys David and Jonathan, has been successfully treading the parental path.

21
Gerald Priestland

*'I am only a poor drunken English
journalist, the religious affairs
correspondent of the BBC.'*

*Gerald Francis Priestland, born 26 February 1927, married
1949 Sylvia Rhodes, two sons, two daughters; BBC correspondent New Delhi 1954–58, Washington 1958–61, Beirut
1961–65, news presenter 1970–76, religious affairs correspondent 1977–82; publications*: America: the Changing
Nation *1968*, The Future of Violence *1976*, Yours Faithfully
(two volumes) 1979, 1981, Priestland's Progress *1981, The
Case Against God 1984*, Something Understood *1986*, The
Unquiet Suitcase *1988; died 20 June 1991, aged 64.*

Gerry Priestland, best known for his highly entertaining
talks as the BBC's religious affairs correspondent, started
his broadcasting career as an obituarist. When he was a
newly married trainee he spent some six months preparing brief notices of the great and the good to be used
in news bulletins. At the age of 22, one of the last things
he did before leaving what he called 'the death department' was to draft his own obituary. He quoted the Archbishop of Canterbury as saying, 'This plucky little
mortician made a living out of dying, but death got him
down.' He later wrote, 'It is one I shall not be around to
hear myself, and in any case obits are revised annually by

my successors.' It undoubtedly had been revised for the BBC's news broadcasts on 20 June 1991, when he died at the age of 64.

Priestland was one of the first six graduates recruited for training by the BBC's News Division. During the war he had won a classics scholarship to Charterhouse, where he was known as the school atheist. From there he was awarded a top open history scholarship to New College. At Oxford his mentors included Isaiah Berlin and Naomi Mitchison, but more important for his future life was the meeting with Sylvia Rhodes, a chestnut-haired student at the Ruskin School of Art, the sister of a school friend of his, and later his partner in a long and very happy marriage.

When Priestland had virtually finished his autobiography *Something Understood*, published in 1986, he read of the death of his first BBC boss, Tahu Hole, the New Zealand Editor of the News Division (see Hole, pp. 123–33). He just had time, he told me, to delete what he had already written and substitute what he really thought of that egregious man.

Tahu – a Maori name – was a monster in every sense. I am sure that he was kind to his wife and his dog, but amongst his staff he inspired nothing but terror, exuding a sinister aroma of power as if he knew something to the discredit of each one of them, as I suppose he took care to do. He took good care to make no operational decisions himself for which he might be blamed if things went wrong.

After five years as a subeditor Priestland had applied to be considered for appointment as a foreign correspondent. He was given the traditional excellent experience of working in France for a few months under the tutelage of Thomas Cadett, the great Paris correspondent first of *The Times* and then of the BBC. Priestland was then summoned by Tahu Hole and told he was being sent to New Delhi. It was typical of Hole that he refused to send Priestland's family to join him until he had proved himself in the post six months later. At 26 he was the youngest man ever appointed as a BBC foreign correspondent, but because Hole had not been sure of his judgement Sylvia had to bear her second child while Gerry was the other side of the globe.

In the subcontinent Priestland by no means restricted himself to Delhi. He sent memorable dispatches from Peshawar, Kathmandu, Goa and what was then East Pakistan, now Bangladesh. One, in his familiar self-deprecating manner, told of how he was taken tiger hunting by an Indian friend. After a night in an unlit draughty resthouse all they saw in the thick and menacing jungle were 'a tabby cat, two man-eating rabbits and some dangerous looking peacocks'. In the end his friend lost his temper and shot a sitting snipe. 'Poor thing, it practically disintegrated. His gun was loaded for a tiger.'

Priestland was a BBC foreign correspondent for altogether sixteen years. In 1958 he transferred to Washington as the number two to Christopher Serpell, who had succeeded me there. He replaced the legendary Douglas Willis, who eventually drank himself to death in Nairobi. Traditionally the Washington number two was the run-about man who covered stories all over the United States. In San Francisco Priestland witnessed the execution in a gas chamber of a convicted rapist. Excursions to the South were for stories about civil rights and school integration. He covered the Kennedy/Nixon presidential election campaign of 1960. Priestland's eve-of-poll article in *The Listener* was headlined 'Kennedy to win by a narrow margin.' Shortly after that correct forecast – a majority of

100,000 in a vote of over 67 million – the Priestland family was transferred to Beirut. They then had three children and a fourth on the way.

Originally the BBC's Middle Eastern correspondent had been situated in Cairo. After the office was closed at the time of Suez Beirut was substituted. It was chosen for its convenience as a base rather than as a major news source in itself. Priestland was constantly on the road, or rather in the air, covering stories in Saudi Arabia, Iraq, Turkey, Syria, Iran and Egypt to the neglect of his family. Soon he decided that the family must come first, and requested a transfer back home.

He was assigned to television news at Alexandra Palace and was on duty there on Monday, 20 April 1964, the ill-fated day on which BBC2 was due to start. It had been planned to transmit on the brand new standards of 625 lines in the Ultra High Frequency band. BBC1 and ITV were still using 405 lines in the Very High Frequency bands. A publicity gimmick of a mother kangaroo with a baby emerging from its pouch had been used to remind viewers they would need new aerials and modern sets to receive the new channel.

BBC1 was scheduled to be transmitting the magazine programme *Tonight* at 7.20 p.m., the time designated for the start of BBC2. *Tonight* had included a kangaroo, due to watch the start of the new channel with Cliff Michelmore. Shortly before 7 p.m., as *Tonight* was ending its rehearsal at Lime Grove, there was a massive power failure which plunged most of western London, including Buckingham Palace and the House of Commons, into darkness. The tube trains stopped running. Nothing could be broadcast from Lime Grove or the new 625-line studios in Television Centre. However, the transmitter at Crystal Palace to the south and the news studios at Alexandra Palace to the north, also equipped for 625 lines, fortunately still had power. Thus at 7.20 p.m., it fell to Priestland not only to announce the start of BBC2, and explain why its promised programme of *Kiss Me Kate* could not take place, but also to explain to BBC1 viewers why they were not receiving their expected fare. He did it with elegance and humour.

Meanwhile the production team of *Panorama* at Lime Grove were desperately heading for Alexandra Palace with cans of film and studio guests to try to mount the programme from there. As they fled in the dark one after another bumped into the large and surly kangaroo stuck outside the non-working scenery lift.

Less than a year later Priestland returned to Washington as chief correspondent, with the late Leonard Parkin, and then Charles Wheeler, as his partner. He marched through Alabama with Martin Luther King and covered the gruesome news of 1968 which saw the assassinations of both King and Robert Kennedy, and American campuses set aflame by Vietnam protesters.

Back in England he had various news outlets in both television and radio (which was his real love) until he suddenly had a nervous breakdown. He was cured by his wife Sylvia, and by a psychiatrist, and by what he was convinced was a third healer. He started going to the Quaker meetings at Hampstead and listened to the Friends' message that there is something of God in everyone. He became an active Quaker, and in the course of time became the BBC's religious affairs correspondent. He soon built up a large and devoted following for his talks on Saturday mornings *Yours Faithfully*, which took the place of Radio 4's *Thought for the Day*. They brought him more listeners' letters each day, he said, than he would receive in Washington in a year. They combined wisdom with humour, and compassion with style. In

Radio 4's annual popularity contest for Man of the Year he was once the runner-up to Prince Charles, beating the Pope.

As religious affairs correspondent he covered the two papal elections of 1978. Irreverently he enjoyed recalling how he nearly lost his life one evening in Rome, when he and a colleague were staggering home somewhat tight. They were obstructing a car which hooted at them. As it overtook them Priestland gave it a loud thump on the roof. Four men jumped out, drawing revolvers. Priestland immediately flung up his hands with the words: 'Don't shoot, don't shoot. I am only a poor drunken English journalist, the religious affairs correspondent of the BBC!'

After retiring from the BBC Gerry Priestland was offered a number of different pulpits: two television series on TVS called *Priestland Right and Wrong* and a weekly spot on Terry Wogan's Radio 2 show, answering listeners' doubts and queries as well as writing newspaper columns. After his death, like Reith, Dimbleby and Wheldon, he has had an annual series of lectures established in his memory, in his case dealing with religious subjects. He was in every sense a good man.

22

John Freeman

'Courteous searching questions'

John Freeman, PC 1966, MBE 1943, born 19 February 1915, married 1st 1938 Elizabeth Johnston, 2nd 1948 Margaret Kerr (died 1957), one adopted daughter, 3rd 1962 Catherine Wheeler, two sons one daughter, 4th 1976 Judith Mitchell, two daughters; advertising consultant 1937–40; active service 1940–45; MP (Labour), Watford division of Herts 1945–50, borough of Watford 1950–56; Parliamentary Private Secretary to Secretary of State for War 1945–46, Financial Secretary, War Office 1946, Parliamentary Under-Secretary of State for War 1947, Parliamentary Secretary, Ministry of Supply, 1947–51; assistant editor, New Statesman *1951–58, deputy editor 1958–60, editor 1961–65; chairman,* Press Conference *1954,* Panorama *1955,* Face to Face *1959–62; British High Commissioner in India 1965–68, British Ambassador in Washington 1969–71; chairman: London Weekend Television Ltd 1971–84, Hutchinson Ltd 1978–82, ITN 1976–81; Governor, BFI 1976–82; vice-president, Royal Television Society 1975–85 (Gold Medal 1981); Visiting Professor of International Relations at the University of California at Los Angeles 1985–90; retired.*

Conservative Members of Parliament who lose ministerial office or are defeated at a General Election tend to go into commerce or industry. Labour Members, by contrast, usually head for journalism or broadcasting. John Freeman was a case in point. He entered Parliament, at the age of 30, as Labour Member for Watford when the Attlee government was swept into office shortly before the end of the Second World War.

As a new backbencher Freeman was given the honour of seconding the Humble Address welcoming King George VI's Speech from the Throne which opened the session. With his good looks, his bright auburn hair and his upright bearing, he cut a fine figure in his major's uniform, decorated with the military MBE, and he made a strong impression on the House. He spoke fluently and effectively, as might be expected of a barrister's eldest son who had been educated at Westminster and Brasenose College, Oxford, and who had made his living in advertising for three years before he joined up.

John Freeman was immediately appointed Parliamentary Private Secretary to the Secretary of State for War. He climbed rapidly up the political ladder, becoming Financial Secretary and Parliamentary Under-Secretary at the War Office, Leader of the United Kingdom Defence Mission to Burma, and finally Parliamentary Secretary at the Ministry of Supply. In April 1951 there was a sudden change. Hugh Gaitskell, the Labour Chancellor of the Exchequer, imposed charges on National Health Service spectacles and false teeth in order to help pay for Britain's part in the Korean war. Two Cabinet Ministers, Aneurin Bevan and Harold Wilson, and a junior Minister, John Freeman, resigned from the government in protest. It was the beginning of the Bevanite split which ravaged the Labour Party for many years.

Even before he resigned, John Freeman had been

involved in discussions with Kingsley Martin, the long-term editor of the *New Statesman and Nation*. This was then the bible of the intellectual left and of the colonial independence movements. Martin was a brilliant journalist with a flair for attracting interesting contributors, if a somewhat erratic political thinker. He was interested in grooming Freeman for succession to his editorial chair, in preference to other contenders such as Richard Crossman, H. N. Brailsford and Basil Davidson. Freeman accepted Martin's offer to supplement his salary as an ordinary MP by becoming assistant editor of the *New Statesman*.

He appeared occasionally as one of the panel of journalists on *Press Conference* and, after 1955, when he gave up his seat in Parliament, he became an interviewer on *Panorama*, along with Christopher Chataway and Woodrow Wyatt. One item on *Panorama* was a report by Woodrow Wyatt which exposed an election fraud in the ballot for officers in the communist-led Electrical Trades Union. The union demanded that its president, Frank Foulkes, be allowed to appear on *Panorama* to reply. John Freeman interviewed him particularly skilfully. Far from being a rebuttal, the interview confirmed skullduggery. I was watching the programme in a viewing room with two of the hard-line union officers who had accompanied Foulkes. 'We should never have allowed him to appear,' one said to the other.

Kingsley Martin, who was not a good broadcaster, was envious of the success of many of his friends on television: Malcolm Muggeridge, Bob Boothby, A. J. P. Taylor and John Freeman. He indicated to Freeman that if he wanted to succeed him as editor of the *New Statesman* he should pay more attention to the magazine and less to *Panorama*. Accordingly John gave up his *Panorama* work and for a while restricted his *Press Conference* appearances.

Several of the producers recruited to Television Talks from the External Services were keen to mount programmes that were television versions of series they had successfully made for radio. Hugh Burnett at Bush House had produced *Personal Call*, a series of in-depth personal interviews conducted at their homes by Dr Stephen Black with well-known personalities such as Lord Birkett and Evelyn Waugh. Burnett wanted to reproduce *Personal Call* on television with a different interviewer. I rejected his suggestion of Randolph Churchill whose behaviour was too unpredictable for live television at that time, and he chose John Freeman on the evidence of his skill as a questioner on *Press Conference* and *Panorama*. The television series was to be called *Face to Face* and would alternate on Sunday evenings with *Monitor*.

The guests on *Face to Face* were a remarkable cross-section of the leading world figures in the mid-twentieth century. Interesting public men and women subjected themselves to a new kind of questioning which extracted from them, by examination in public, their background and beliefs rather than their views on current topics. They included Dame Edith Sitwell, Adam Faith, Augustus John, Stirling Moss and Cecil Beaton, as well as Martin Luther King and Adlai Stevenson from the USA, Sir Roy Welensky and Jomo Kenyatta from Africa, King Hussein of Jordan, Otto Klemperer, Carl Jung, Simone Signoret, Nubar Gulbenkian and many others. Altogether there were thirty-five, between 4 February 1959 and 18 March 1962.

Face to Face opened on to a specially commissioned sketch of the guest drawn by Feliks Topolski, accompanied by the first bars of Berlioz's *Les Francs Juges*. It then mixed to a close-up of the person in the studio seated in the same pose against a background of black curtains. He or she was seated on a platform, slightly higher than John Freeman, a wise psychological move on Burnett's part. Only the guest was seen full-face, usually in a tight close-up. The back of Freeman's head was sometimes shown, but rarely. The camera was used as a second interrogator.

Burnett's first guests were those he had already produced in *Personal Call*. He knew they would perform well, and judicious use of the old transcripts provided John Freeman with better than average research for his probing but not abrasive interviews. Like Sue Lawley today, Freeman combined courtesy with persistence. He had an attractive voice, and usually managed to conduct his searching questioning on *Face to Face* without giving any impression of harassment.

One exception was his famous programme with Gilbert Harding (see Harding, p. 119). Another was his interview with Tony Hancock, which led to a strong friendship between Tony and himself. Some people criticised John for being 'hostile' to the nation's favourite comic, and for bullying and exposing him in an unkindly way. John defended himself by saying,

'Well, I hope I did expose him – that, after all, is the object of *Face to Face*; but "hostility" and "bullying" – no. I asked Tony searching questions, and, instead of turning them aside with a stream of wisecracks as most top-flight comics would have done (and Tony is entirely capable of doing if he'd wanted to), he took them seriously. He pondered them; he hesitated; and then – sometimes I think painfully – he answered with unexpected candour and without any trace of a public idol's vanity.'

When King Hussein came to Lime Grove to appear on *Face to Face* I was sitting at the back of the studio with his two Jordanian bodyguards. There was a sudden moment of tenseness, and they seemed to be reaching for their revolvers, when Freeman had the temerity to ask the King whether he had come to England to look for a new wife.

Sometimes the programme ran into trouble. In Kenya Jomo Kenyatta suddenly took umbrage. Burnett had arranged a luncheon beforehand, serving chicken which was said by Kenyatta's secretary to be his favourite dish. When the BBC's representative in Nairobi mentioned that they had succeeded in getting him some chicken, Kenyatta declared angrily that he would not be bought with a chicken and stormed out. He was lured back when it was made clear that he was in danger of offending not only the BBC but also – and this was more serious – the deputy editor of the *New Statesman*. Freeman had just been promoted and Kenyatta had previously stayed with Kingsley Martin at his country cottage in Essex.

Evelyn Waugh provided a different kind of problem. After taking part in Hugh Burnett's *Personal Call* programme he had suffered the breakdown described in *The Ordeal of Gilbert Pinfold*, which gave an account of the author's preoccupations with questioning voices and sounds in the air. He did not want to appear on *Face to Face*, but when Hugh Burnett telephoned, instead of giving a straightforward refusal, Waugh said, 'You couldn't afford my fee.' 'What is your fee?' Burnett asked. 'Two hundred and fifty guineas,' said Waugh. Burnett called his bluff by agreeing immediately.

The standard fee for appearances on *Face to Face* was then 100 guineas, a high figure for those days. The first guest on the programme, Lord Birkett, had originally been offered a measly 15 guineas owing to a mistake by the bookings department. We arranged not to send the standard contract form to Waugh but wrote him a letter confirming the special fee of 250 guineas to include all rights, and got him to sign an acceptance. *Face to Face* always had at least one repeat on BBC television and was usually sold overseas. With the normal residual rights all the other guests received in all well over 250 guineas for their appearances. Evelyn Waugh's bravado therefore earned him less than anyone else, and extracts from the programme could later be freely used, for instance to promote *Brideshead Revisited*.

Waugh was in an aggressive mood before the programme. 'The name is Waugh – not Wuff!' he said when Freeman was introduced. 'But I called you Mr Waugh,' John Freeman smiled. 'No, no, I distinctly heard you say "Wuff",' Waugh persisted, with what obviously was gamesmanship.

As well as conducting the *Face to Face* interviews John Freeman frequently acted as chairman of the panel of journalists on *Press Conference*. In 1960 the Guild of Television Producers and Directors, now BAFTA, awarded him the title Television Personality of the Year, and he received many new programme offers.

In 1961 he finally succeeded Kingsley Martin as editor of the *New Statesman*. Four years later Harold Wilson, one of the colleagues with whom he had resigned from the Attlee government in 1951, and by now Prime Minister himself, appointed him to be British High Commissioner in India. From the Indian point of view it was an imaginative choice. Kingsley Martin had been a close friend of Nehru, and the *New Statesman* was highly regarded by the Indian Establishment.

John Freeman has been a much married man. His first marriage ended in divorce in 1948. His second wife died of cancer in 1957. In 1962 he married Catherine Wheeler, the former wife of Charles Wheeler, the BBC's news correspondent in India. Previously Charles had been a producer on *Panorama*. Catherine Dove had directed *Panorama* and *Press Conference* before briefly being the first producer of *Monitor*. So they had all been working in the Television Talks department together. Once John had settled in at the High Commission in New Dehli Catherine and their three children flew out to join him. I was on the same plane, on my way to advise the Indian government on how to establish a television service. For most of the flight I had one or another little Freeman sitting on my knee.

Soon after we arrived the Freemans and I all attended an Indian government dinner at which we ran into Laksmi Jha, an old Indian friend who had been on the committee of the Cambridge Union the term I was President. He was then the Prime Minister's private secretary, and had previously served Moraji Desai, the dictatorial Indian Finance Minister, in the same capacity. He recalled that we had all last met at Lime Grove when Desai had appeared on *Press Conference*. 'You,' Jha said to the High Commissioner, 'were the chairman of the journalists. You,' he turned to Catherine, 'were the producer, and you,' to me, 'were the head of the department. And I have never seen Moraji Desai under such discipline before or since!'

John Freeman was a great success in India. On principle he declined the customary High Commissioner's knighthood and instead he was made a Privy Counsellor after he had been there a year. In 1969 he was promoted to become British Ambassador in Washington, a post frequently held by men who are not career diplomats.

The Washington chapter of the National Academy of Television Arts and Sciences consisted almost entirely of people working in the news and public affairs field, for the American entertainment programmes tended to be made elsewhere. The members were delighted to discover that the new British ambassador and his wife were television experts, and soon inquired whether the Embassy would care to mount an evening honouring British television at which a BBC and an ITN public affairs programme would be shown.

John immediately recognised that this was a bid for a free party but felt it might be worth doing. He rang me up in New York (I was then the BBC's representative in the US) and asked whether the BBC would like to provide something. Kenneth Clark's *Civilisation* had just started on BBC2 and I got sent out a copy of its fourth episode, based on Florence and filmed in splendid colour with lovely music. ITN provided a news documentary in black and white which put them at a monstrously unfair disadvantage. I also persuaded the Freemans to invite the heads of the main art galleries in Washington to come along to see *Civilisation*. The next day the National Art Gallery contracted to buy it for non-theatric showings and opened up a vast new market for BBC Enterprises.

The Foreign Office had offered Catherine Freeman a secretary with an impeccable social background but she preferred the sort of down-to-earth, supremely practical secretary she was accustomed to working alongside at the BBC. She chose Judith Mitchell, the daughter of another very talented producer in Television Talks, Denis Mitchell, whose documentaries won the Italia Prize and many other awards. At the end of his ambassadorship in 1971 John left Catherine for Judith, who became his fourth wife. He then embarked on yet another career as a highly successful executive in Independent Television.

Face to Face remains one of the best series of interviews ever mounted by the BBC.

23

Robin Day

'He is like a gruff teddy bear,
occasionally cantankerous but never
afraid to laugh at himself.'

Robin Day, Kt 1981, born 24 October 1923, married 1965
Katherine Ainslie (marriage dissolved 1986), two sons; Royal
Artillery 1943–47; president, Oxford Union 1950; barrister
1952–53; British Information Services, Washington 1953–54;
freelance broadcaster 1954–55; BBC radio talks producer 1955,
newscaster and parliamentary correspondent, ITN 1955–59,
reporter: Roving Report *(ITN),* Tell the People *(ITN),*
Under Fire *(Granada);* News Chronicle *columnist 1959;*
Liberal candidate, Hereford, 1959; BBC television programmes:
Panorama, Gallery, People to Watch, Daytime, 24 Hours,
Midweek, Sunday Debate, Talk-in, Newsday, Question
Time; *radio programmes:* It's Your Line, Election Call, The
World at One; *chairman, Hansard Society 1981–83; Guild of*
TV Producers' Merit Award, Personality of the Year 1957,
Richard Dimbleby Award for factual television 1974, Broad-
casting Press Guild Award for Question Time *1980, Judges*
Award for 30 years TV journalism 1985; publications: Tele-
vision: A Personal Report *1961;* The Case for Televising
Parliament *1963;* Day by Day: A Dose of My Own
Hemlock *1975;* Grand Inquisitor *1989; . . . But with Respect*
1993; honorary degrees from Exeter, Keele and Essex Uni-
versities.

In the autumn of 1949 two members of the Oxford Union Society's debating team called in at my office in Washington. Both were ex-servicemen. One was a 25 year-old sandy-haired graduate, Geoffrey Johnson Smith, at that time a socialist, now Sir Geoffrey and a distinguished Conservative MP.

The other was Robin Day, slightly older than Geoffrey, but still an undergraduate. He had taken time off from his legal studies at St Edmund Hall to experience this debating tour on the recommendation of his tutor, Zelman Cowen, later Governor-General of Australia, Provost of Oriel College and chairman of the Visnews Trustees. It was wise advice, for the debating skills Robin refined in verbal duels at some forty-five American universities enabled him to make such a strong impression at the Oxford Union on his return that he was elected President by a large majority.

I, too, had been on a talking tour in the United States after presiding at the Cambridge Union, so we had much in common to discuss, particularly the variety of transport required to get you from one campus to the next and the curious places where you were sometimes expected to sleep. Robin was considerably fatter in those days than he is now. He was amusing and had lots of vitality. I enjoyed meeting him.

What struck me about both Robin and Geoffrey was how very much they seemed to be relishing the United States. At the end of their tour Geoffrey took a job with the British Information Services in San Francisco and married a beautiful American psychiatrist. Later he worked in Television Talks (see Michelmore, p. 209).

The next time I saw Robin was in September 1953. He was then also working for the British Information Services, but in the Washington office which happened to be next door to the BBC in the National Press building. In the intervening four years he had taken his degree at Oxford, been called to the Bar, and won two Middle Temple scholarships, including the greatly valued Harmsworth. Between them they had paid for his pupillage and provided him with a bare living. However, at the age of 29 he had decided to give up a legal career. He was not enjoying it, and it was not paying him enough.

Robin Day heard that the late Charles Campbell, the director of the BIS Washington office, whom he had met during his debating tour, was looking for an assistant. Charlie Campbell was a well-known figure in Anglo-American journalistic circles. He was a hard-drinking, womanising extrovert with a razor-sharp mind. He looked like Colonel Blimp and was the last person you would take for a British civil servant. He was well liked, and trusted, by American journalists of all political persuasions.

In the few months that we overlapped in Washington I often wondered why Robin had decided to take on that job as Charlie Campbell's assistant. He counted as locally recruited staff, which meant he had to pay his own fare across the Atlantic. He did not enjoy diplomatic status or allowances, and he found the work dull and unrewarding. But gradually he began to enjoy life more. He met some of the journalists and observed that Elmer Davis, one of the wisest and best of the American commentators, always wore the same bow tie on television, knowledge that he tucked away for future use. He got to know some of the Congressmen on Capitol Hill and began to get involved in politics, which has always been his first love and which is Washington's main industry.

By that time I had returned to England. The following

year Robin also came back and wrote to me seeking a job in Television Talks. I did not think that his track record so far qualified him for television production work but sought a second opinion by getting Grace Wyndham Goldie to see him. She was of the same mind and referred him to radio current affairs. Perhaps we were wrong. But I still think that Robin would not have been as effective producing for television as he shortly became appearing on it.

After brief spells of work on *Topic for Tonight* as a broadcaster and *At Home and Abroad* as a radio producer, Robin was tipped off in June 1955 that Aidan Crawley, the designated first editor of Independent Television News, was advertising in the Inns of Court for a 'newscaster'. Crawley had recently been presenting a major current affairs series, *Viewfinder*, for Television Talks. He and *Viewfinder's* producer James Bredin were at that time organising the start of news on ITV.

Aidan Crawley was one of the outstanding cricketers of our time. He had played for Oxford and for Kent. In one first-class match he hit ten sixes, and he had been president of the MCC. But he can never have batted on an easier wicket than when he challenged the television news programmes provided from Alexandra Palace in 1955 by Tahu Hole (see Hole, p. 130). The BBC newsreaders, and they were strictly 'readers' and not 'casters', were completely tied into the announcing traditions of Broadcasting House. Hole decreed that their faces were not to be shown. When there was no moving film for the voice-over a still picture was substituted. When all else failed the BBC's coat of arms was used.

That denial of visual communication – so different from the journalism practised at Lime Grove by the *Sportsview* and current affairs programmes – was only abandoned three weeks before the start of Crawley's competitive service. From then, BBC news was presented in a much more informal style by either Christopher Chataway or Robin Day.

Chris Chataway was a natural choice for the screen. Handsome, 24 years old, he was already famous for helping to set the pace for Roger Bannister's first four-minute mile. This had shortly been followed by his own dramatic victory in the London versus Moscow athletics at White City. He beat the European champion Vladimir Kuts in a thrilling 5,000-metre race which broke the world record by a remarkable five seconds.

The other newscaster was less obviously acceptable. Robin Day's spectacles were a drawback. Aidan Crawley thought that his acerbic tone and aggressive manner might irritate some people, as it did Sidney Bernstein, the head of Granada Television, but felt he was the ideal complement to Chataway's film star looks and boyish charm. Crawley said he chose Robin Day because he thought the astringency in his manner and voice would make him a good interviewer. Sir Geoffrey Cox, who succeeded Crawley as editor of ITN, considered that Day looked the part of a prosecuting counsel.

Robin Day's bestselling books of memoirs, *Television: A Personal Report* (1961), *Day by Day: A Dose of My Own Hemlock* (1975) and *Grand Inquisitor* (1989) as well as ... *But with Respect – Memorable Television Interviews with Statesmen and Parliamentarians* (1993), have told his own story of how, after a difficult start, he developed his particular style of interviewing, and who were the world figures he questioned after he ceased to be a newscaster and became a political reporter in the year of Suez.

He has described his four years with ITN from 1955 to 1959 as the happiest in his television career. He enjoyed making film reports from abroad acting as his own director. In 1957 he was chosen as Personality of the Year by the Guild of Television Producers and Directors for his news work. Notable programme successes in that period included an exclusive talk with President Nasser after Eden's ill-fated Suez venture, the first 'tough' interview with a Prime Minister – Harold Macmillan in 1958 – and, in the same year, the live commentary on the State Opening of Parliament the first time it was televised. He chose a deliberately different style from that of Richard Dimbleby on the BBC.

Robin would dearly have liked to become a parliamentarian, though he soon abandoned his early commitment to the Liberal Party, in whose interest he contested Hereford in the General Election of 1959. The Liberals then had an allocation of two Election Broadcasts on television. One took the form of a solo appeal by the leader of the party, Jo Grimond.

The other consisted of short statements by five candidates for marginal seats who were thought to have a good chance of winning. John Arlott, the splendid cricket commentator, who was contesting Epping, acted as moderator. The others were Glyn Tegai Hughes, later a BBC National Governor for Wales, Mark Bonham Carter, son of the redoubtable Lady Violet (who was Asquith's daughter, Grimond's mother-in-law and the vice-president of the party), Renée Soskin, the sister of Lord Beloff, and Robin Day.

Mrs Soskin was the only one who had not broadcast before, and in the rehearsal she delivered her prepared remarks as though she were addressing an audience in the Royal Albert Hall. On our way down to the hospitality room during what was known as 'line-up' I urged John Arlott to have a word with her. 'I wonder if I may be allowed to give you a tip about broadcasting that I've always found helpful?' he asked her, 'When I look at that microphone or that camera lens, I just think to myself that I am talking to someone's mum. Not,' he added emphatically to Mark Bonham Carter, 'not *your* mum!'

Lady Violet came to speak for Robin at Hereford but neither he nor any of the other four was elected. Robin had had to give up his job at ITN while he was actively nursing his constituency, and had temporarily been writing political journalism for the *News Chronicle*. At one stage I telephoned him to say that if he was not successful in getting into Parliament I would very much like him to join *Panorama*. I made the same offer to Ludovic Kennedy. We had already tempted Robin's original ITN colleague Chris Chataway to join *Panorama* about a year after independent television started. *Panorama* was then at the zenith of its reputation. Chris had been an excellent reporter for *Panorama* (see Jacob, p. 99). But at that time he had set his sights on a political career as a Conservative, first with the London County Council, and from 1959 as MP for Lewisham North.

Woodrow Wyatt and Geoffrey Johnson Smith had also successfully stood for Parliament in 1959, so we had vacancies for new reporters with an interest in politics. For the next few years *Panorama* had its strongest team, headed by Richard Dimbleby and including James Mossman, Robert Kee and John Morgan as well as Robin and Ludovic Kennedy, augmented in 1963 by Michael Charlton.

Panorama at that time was a topical magazine covering several of the subjects uppermost in the news rather than devoting itself to a single theme. It also took very seriously its self-imposed obligation to be 'television's window on the world', with many reports from overseas. Robin himself made several from Africa as well as from Cuba and the United States.

Gradually, however, he came to prefer live studio appearances to reports recorded on film. This was not because he is a poor reporter. He is a very good one; but what he loves best is arguing. At dinner parties or a lunch at the Garrick Club he will often make some outrageous assertion just to get a good argument going. And it was his delight in political debate that gave him such a strong position as a challenging interviewer of political leaders. As the left-wing Member of Parliament for West Fife, William Hamilton, put it, 'Members are more afraid of Robin Day than any member of this House.'

There is a lot of gamesmanship in the one-to-one political interview. Robin modified his originally abrasive style and gradually learnt that the best way to handle a politician who evades answering an awkward question is not to hector but to repeat the question in different and slightly politer terms, with apologies for not making himself clear the first time, thus ensuring the sympathy of the television audience stays with the questioner and does not switch to the politician who is apparently being harassed.

Various people developed different ways of handling Robin's questions. Sir John Nott, the Secretary of State for Defence, angrily walked out of the studio during the Conservative Party Conference at Brighton when he was called a 'here today and gone tomorrow politician'. Margaret Thatcher would steamroller the point she was determined to make, regardless of the question Robin had put. James Callaghan had an effective way of stonewalling a verbal googly. 'I really don't know, Robin. What do you think should be done?'

What made these set-piece political interviews into political events was essentially Robin's instinct for identifying the key point, the gut issue, and going for it without fear or favour. He has always shown outstanding courage in being prepared to ask questions from which others would shrink. A classic case was his long interview with Lord Lambton, the disgraced Air Force Minister who had resigned from the government and from Parliament after his relationship with call girls had been exposed in the press. Robin was somewhat inhibited by the presence of Lord Lambton's young schoolboy son in the room during the interview.

Another bold and unusual interview was with Jan Morris after her sex change. James Morris had been an undergraduate contemporary of Robin and was later one of the reporters on *Panorama* before he went to Casablanca for the change of sex operation. Robin handled the interview sensitively.

His life has had its share of disappointments and sadness. His marriage to a brilliant Australian lawyer ended in divorce by mutual consent. One of his two sons suffered appalling injury when he fell, at the age of $4\frac{1}{2}$, some 25 feet into a concrete vehicle yard at the London Zoo. Robin himself was mugged in the street and had his jaw broken. He broke his pelvis while skiing. After he had undergone bypass surgery he managed to give up those smelly cigars that used to permeate the *Panorama* office at Lime Grove, without showing adverse withdrawal symptoms.

Robin Day was an early advocate of televising the proceedings of Parliament, arguing that the nation's main forum of debate and decision should not be cut off from the nation's main medium of communication. He argued in favour of it in letters to *The Times* in the late 1950s and in a pamphlet he wrote for the Hansard Society and published at his own expense.

As Paul Fox has said, Robin is wonderful on election night. His set-piece interviews with the political leaders have always managed to be incisive, despite the fact that they have often come at the end of a long night's feverish activity which in turn has been the climax of a long period of *Election Call* programmes on radio and television or both in which he has acted as the tribune of enfranchised listeners and viewers.

Question Time, which started on 25 September 1979, was the ideal platform for Robin Day's love of argument and his ambition to be recognised as an entertainer. It began as a television version of the long-running radio programme *Any Questions?* when the Governors jibbed at Bill Cotton's idea of a five nights a week chat-show with Michael Parkinson as host. A new programme had to be mounted in the Greenwood Theatre, Southwark, and Barbara Maxwell was asked to produce it, using 'Robin Day with some MPs and an audience to ask questions'. Barbara Maxwell persuaded Cabinet Ministers to appear in a programme where they might have to answer questions about the portfolios of their colleagues, and under Robin's felicitous chairmanship it rapidly became an important fixture in BBC1's schedule in its own right. His natural wit and charm were never better displayed.

Question Time also owed a lot to Ann Morley's brilliant camera direction. During the warm-up period before the start of the programme Robin would often refer jocularly to the director as 'my mistress in the gallery', once much to the embarrassment of Ann Morley's mother who had come to watch the show. He was always a favourite with the technical crew. 'He is like a gruff teddy bear,' one of the sound supervisors said, 'occasionally cantankerous but never afraid to laugh at himself and we all loved him.'

Why did Robin abandon *Question Time* after ten years of success? He says the strain on his health was a factor, and he had written the book *Grand Inquisitor* which had some critical things to say about the BBC, particularly about its recent Directors-General. I think he now believes it was a mistake to give up the programme.

He soon won every possible honour in his chosen *métier*. He was the first broadcast journalist to receive a knighthood, on the recommendation of Margaret Thatcher in 1981, though it had slipped her memory when Sir Robin interviewed her in 1983 on *Election Panorama*, and several viewers thought that her forgetful mistake in calling him 'Mr Day' five times was a deliberate snub. He has received honorary degrees from three universities and won every major professional television award. He has interviewed six Prime Ministers and been at the centre of the television coverage of eight General Elections. A gregarious man with a wicked sense of humour, he is socially in great demand. In October 1993, well over two hundred people paid £50 each to attend a charity lunch in celebration of his 70th birthday.

In his book, Sir Robin carefully analysed the role of the Grand Inquisitor, and articulated it very well but because he has established his principles for the major set-piece interview so clearly he may find it difficult to adjust to a new role. He would like to have been Director-General of the BBC. He would like to have earned as much from television as Walter Cronkite in America. He has always wanted to be a star and to command recognition. Hence, among other things, the spotted bow tie. Yet at the same time he has hankered after a high-level managerial job without making any particular preparation for it. He has climbed to the top of his professional tree, but he does not seem to enjoy the view from it. I don't know why.

24

Ludovic Kennedy

*'There seem to be a lot of us Kennedys
around.'*

*Ludovic Henry Coverley Kennedy, born 3 November 1919,
married 1950 Moira Shearer King, one son three daughters;
Midmanship, Sub-Lieutenant, Lieutenant RNVR (1939–45);
Private Secretary and ADC to Governor of Newfoundland
1943–44; librarian, Ashridge Adult Education College 1949;
Rockefeller Foundation Award in Literature 1950; winner,
English Festival of Spoken Poetry 1953; editor,* First Reading,
*BBC Third Programme 1953–54; British Council, lecturer,
Sweden, Finland and Denmark 1955, Belgium and Lux-
embourg 1956; presenter,* Profile, *ATV 1955–56; newscaster,
ITN 1956–58; introducer,* One Stage, *AR 1957,* This Week,
*AR 1958–59; Liberal candidate, Rochdale 1958 and 1959; presi-
dent, National League of Young Liberals 1959–61; joined BBC,
1960; reporter,* Panorama *1960–63; Television Reporters Inter-
national 1963–64; chairman:* Your Verdict *1962,* Your
Witness *1967–70; introducer:* Time Out *1964–65,* The World
at One *1965–66,* The Middle Years, *ABC 1967,* The Nature
of Prejudice, *ATV 1968,* Face the Press, *Tyne-Tees 1968–69,*
Against the Tide, *Yorkshire TV 1969,* Living and Growing,
Grampian TV 1969–70, 24 Hours *1969–72,* Ad Lib *1970–72,*
Midweek *1973–75,* Newsday *1975–76,* A Life with Crime
1979, Change of Direction *1979,* Lord Mountbatten

Remembers *1980*, Did You See? *1980–88*, Timewatch *1984*, Indelible Evidence *1987*, A Gift of the Gab *1989*, Portrait *1989; television films include:* The Sleeping Ballerina, The Singers and the Songs, Scapa Flow, Battleship Bismarck, Life and Death of the Scharnhorst, U-Boat War, Target Tirpitz, The Rise of the Red Navy, Lord Haw-Haw, Coast to Coast, Who Killed the Lindbergh Baby?, Elizabeth: the First Thirty Years, Happy Birthday, Dear Ma'am; *publications:* Sub-Lieutenant *1942*, Nelson's Band of Brothers *1951*, One Man's Meat *1953*, Murder Story *1954*, Ten Rillington Place *1961*, The Trial of Stephen Ward *1964*, Very Lovely People *1969*, Pursuit: the Chase and Sinking of the Bismarck *1973*, A Presumption of Innocence *1975*, Menace: the Life and Death of the Tirpitz *1979*, A Book of Railway Journeys *1980*, A Book of Sea Journeys *1981*, A Book of Air Journeys *1982*, The Airman and the Carpenter *1985*, On My Way to the Club *1989*.

Ludovic Kennedy joined *Panorama* at the same time and for the same reason as Robin Day. He too had been standing as a Liberal candidate in the 1959 General Election, and had had to give up his job in independent television while he was nursing his constituency, Rochdale. Ludo's immediately previous post was presenting Associated-Rediffusion's weekly current affairs programme *This Week*, a magazine for which he had no great fondness or respect. We lunched together before the election and I made him an offer to come to *Panorama* if he failed to get into the House of Commons.

I had been invited to watch *This Week* being transmitted from its Kingsway studio earlier that year, on 1 April to be precise. Peter Sellers was there with Ludo, wearing a red wig and a beard. They were rehearsing an April Fool hoax with Sellers playing the part of a Hungarian explorer who had just returned from the Himalayas where he had been the first European to see the Abominable Snowman, photograph it and bring back tufts of its hair. Suddenly, only a few minutes before transmission, Sellers declared that he would prefer to play the part as a Scottish professor with a pawky accent. Unfazed, Ludo Kennedy quickly introduced Sellers to viewers as Professor Grant-Hamilton of the University of Camelford. The deadpan interview was very funny.

Before moving to *This Week* Ludo had also been a news-caster on ITN. He had had to give that up the first time he stood for Rochdale, at a by-election in 1958. Previously he had not been particularly interested in party politics, although his father had been a Conservative agent and his cousin Bob Boothby was one of the best-known back-bench MPs, owing to his frequent appearances on tele-vision. Ludo had decided to stand as a Liberal at that by-election partly because he felt passionately that Sir Anthony Eden's Suez venture had been a terrible mistake, and partly because he was attracted by the personality of the late Jo Grimond who had become leader of the party in 1956.

Ludovic Kennedy did well in that by-election, not well enough to win but sufficiently well to drive the Con-servatives, the previous holders of the seat, into third place. He was greatly helped by the fact that his face was familiar, after two years of newscasting for ITN. He was also vigorously supported by his beautiful red-haired wife, the dancer and film star Moira Shearer, then at the height of her fame.

In 1950, at what was described as the 'wedding of the year', the glamorous ballerina had married the naval hero's son. Ludo's father was indeed a naval hero. Captain E. C. Kennedy had had to leave the Royal Navy in 1922 after a court martial for not taking adequate measures to suppress an outbreak of insubordination during a period of industrial unrest. However, at the start of the Second World War, he had been reinstated and given command of an old passenger liner which had been converted into a semi-armed merchant cruiser, HMS *Rawalpindi*. She had defied the two powerful battlecruisers *Scharnhorst* and *Gneisenau* in a heroic defeat against odds. It was the first surface naval action of the Second World War and Ludo was still a midshipman when his father was killed. King George VI subsequently granted his mother a grace and favour apartment at Hampton Court Palace.

Ludovic Kennedy's relationship with his domineering mother was not a particularly happy one, as he revealed in his candid autobiography *On My Way to the Club*. He came from a more privileged background than most of his fellow television presenters. His Scottish ancestors included the Lords Kennedy, later Marquesses of Ailsa, and his mother was the daughter of an eleventh baronet. He had been educated at Eton and had organised an exotic stunt during his last week there. It involved hiring a light aircraft to take four friends and himself to Le Touquet between college rollcalls, to drink champagne and, they hoped, to cover the cost of the flight by winnings at the casino.

He had a year at Christ Church, Oxford, before war broke out. He immediately enlisted in the navy and took part in exciting forays against the German battleships *Bismarck* and *Tirpitz* and in escorting convoys to Russia. These were chronicled in his first book *Sub-Lieutenant* which also paid an affectionate tribute to his late father. Later in the war he spent a year as ADC to the Governor of Newfoundland.

Once the war was over Ludovic Kennedy returned to

Oxford to finish his studies, and to help found the Writers' Club. He was busily writing books himself after he graduated, while also working as librarian at Ashridge Adult Education College. He published a book on Nelson's captains and broadcast a number of poetry readings on what then was the Third Programme, winning the English Festival of Spoken Poetry competition in 1953. He also lectured for the British Council in Scandinavia and in the Low Countries.

Shortly after their marriage in 1950 the handsome young author and his glamorous ballerina wife visited Hollywood where Moira was due to co-star with Danny Kaye in *Hans Christian Andersen*. Moira's pregnancy with their first child ended that lengthy dancing project, but she did have time to appear instead with James Mason in one of three short films which made up *Story of Three Loves*. Ludo continued his writing career, contributing a number of articles to the *Sunday Times*.

In addition to being a successful author Kennedy had ambitions to become a broadcaster. Soon after the start of ITV he got a number of minor engagements as a presenter. Aidan Crawley gave him an audition as a newscaster and shortly thereafter he was hastily summoned to ITN's headquarters. Chris Chataway was in Edinburgh and Robin Day had gone down with flu. Could he read the two evening bulletins? He stayed for the next two years.

After he joined the *Panorama* team of reporters Ludo presented many film stories from various foreign parts including Saudi Arabia. In May 1960 he and Robin Day joined Richard Dimbleby in Moscow for the special edition of *Panorama* which was mounted in conjunction with the BBC's live coverage of the May Day parade (see Fox, p. 149). They suffered the usual frustrations of reporters being shepherded around by over-zealous

Intourist interpreters, but they still managed to film some very interesting material for the first British magazine programme to visit the Soviet Union.

Two months later *Panorama* reported for the first time from an American political convention – the one at Los Angeles which nominated John F. Kennedy as the Democratic candidate for the Presidency. As a veteran of American political conventions I led a strong team which included Ludo and Robin, the Editor of *Panorama* Michael Peacock, and another member of his production team with strong links to America, David Webster. We also engaged locally a brilliant research assistant who soon was to become a distinguished producer herself, Revel Guest. At a press conference with the nominee where the reporters were asked to identify themselves Ludo began his question by saying 'I am Ludovic Kennedy from the BBC. There seem to be a lot of us Kennedys around.'

When the Democratic National Convention was over we spent a relaxing evening at a Hollywood night-club where Ludo for a while took over the percussion section of the band. Vivien Leigh came in, and immediately went over to embrace the relief drummer. Through his marriage to Moira he felt comfortably at home in the show business world and he enjoyed the company of impresarios and those in the acting profession. Ludo himself also enjoyed acting. In one episode of *Yes Minister* he happily interviewed Sir Humphrey Appleby (Nigel Hawthorne) and he appeared as a newscaster or a television presenter in a number of other programmes.

The next time the two Kennedys met, Ludo was flattered to find that the President knew him to be the author of the recent book about a series of murders in Notting Hill. This was *10 Rillington Place*, a detailed piece of research into the murder of a woman and her baby daughter for which her husband Timothy Evans was wrongfully hanged. Sixteen years later the Queen granted Evans a free pardon. It was Kennedy's book that had cleared his name.

Ludo has always been a campaigner against miscarriages of justice, perhaps as a result of what he regarded as the unfairness of his father's naval court martial. Altogether he has written six books and a play dealing with crimes and with those who he believes were wrongly accused of them. They include books about Stephen Ward, Patrick Meehan, the Portland Spy case and the Luton post office murder.

In 1980 when he was in America he happened to see on television an old lady protesting that her late husband had been innocent, and that with the help of information now available under the Freedom of Information Act she was going to bring an action against the state of New Jersey. She was speaking of Bruno Hauptmann, the German-American carpenter who had been electrocuted in 1936 for the murder of the baby son of Charles Lindbergh, the American national hero who had been the first to fly solo across the Atlantic. This immediately stirred Ludo's concern for cases of apparent miscarriages of justice. With the encouragement of Will Wyatt, then the Head of Documentary Features, he wrote and narrated an hour-long BBC television programme *Who Killed the Lindbergh Baby?* The documentary was later expanded into a book *The Airman and the Carpenter*.

Ludo made several other long documentaries for BBC television. One was a obituary of Admiral Earl Mountbatten which was used after his murder by the IRA. Mountbatten had learnt that a standby obituary was being prepared. He asked that it should take the form of an interview with himself in which he would talk about his life and say what kind of a funeral he would like. It was the first programme made specifically as an obituary to consist of a pre-filmed discussion with the deceased. The film was repeated on the eightieth anniversary of Mountbatten's birth, supplemented with an interview in which the Prince of Wales spoke to Kennedy about his uncle. Ludo also made naval war documentary programmes – *Bismarck*, *Tirpitz*, *Scharnhorst* and *The U-Boat War* and several about great railway journeys.

At different times in what has been a most versatile television career he introduced a wide variety of programmes in the current affairs field, including *24 Hours*, *Midweek*, *Newsday*, and *Tonight*. For eight years Ludo chaired the discussion group which commented on recent television programmes, *Did You See?*. I think it was probably this programme which caused a television critic to write, 'He gives me the impression that he has been good enough to drop by to see if he can lend a hand while on his way to the club' – the comment which provided the title for his autobiography, first published in 1989. In it he revealed, with what some felt was embarrassing candour, his psychological hangups. It also indicated the wide range of his interests outside the world of broadcasting.

These include a passionate concern for the correct use of the English language. I took the chair for him at the Royal Society of Arts where he made a ferocious attack on what he called the 'moronic' use of language by disc jockeys, with the notable exception of Terry Wogan. Another of his concerns is voluntary euthanasia, about which he has written vigorously to the press. Scottish nationalism has always been dear to his heart, but top of the list, and what has given him the greatest personal satisfaction, has been his crusade against miscarriages of justice, particularly where he has successfully exposed tainted evidence or judicial malpractice, and above all where his intervention has released an innocent person from languishing in jail. He has been one of the most respected and popular figures on the television screen. His contribution to the BBC has been a combination of intelligence, style and integrity.

25

Charles Hill

*'Like appointing Rommel to
command the Eighth Army'*

*Charles Hill, Life Peer (Baron Hill of Luton) 1963, PC 1955,
MA, MD, DPH, LLD, born 15 January 1904, married 1931
Marion Spencer Wallace, two sons three daughters; house phys-
ician, London Hospital; London University extension lecturer
in biology; hospital posts in Nottingham and Oxford; secretary,
British Medical Association 1944–50; MP (Lib. & Cons.)
Luton 1950–63, Parliamentary Secretary, Ministry of Food
1951–55, Postmaster-General 1955–57, Chancellor of the
Duchy of Lancaster 1957–61, Minister of Housing and Local
Government and Minister for Welsh Affairs 1961–62; chairman, ITA 1963–67; Chairman, BBC 1967–72; chairman,
Abbey National Building Society and Laporte Industries; publications: What is Osteopathy? 1937; Re-printed Broadcasts
1941–50; Both Sides of the Hill 1964; Behind the Screen
1974; died 23 August 1989 aged 85.*

'I have some bad news for you.' It was 26 July 1967. I was
at the BBC office in New York. The telephone call was
from my boss in London, Donald Stephenson. I braced
myself. 'Lord Hill is going to be the new Chairman of the
BBC,' he said, in sepulchral tones.

Stephenson's reaction was typical of the immediate

shock in Broadcasting House on hearing that the chairman of the ITA and most vigorous protagonist of the rival commercial television system would be transferred overnight to the public service BBC. 'Like appointing Rommel to command the Eighth Army' was the comment that simultaneously occurred to David Attenborough and Robert Lusty, who had been the BBC's acting Chairman since the death in office the previous month of Lord Normanbrook.

It had been a strange afternoon for Lusty. He had been summoned by the Postmaster-General, Edward Short (later Lord Glenamara), and told that the press had got wind of who the Prime Minister Harold Wilson had in mind as Normanbrook's successor. The Queen, Short said, had therefore held an emergency Privy Council meeting at Goodwood racecourse to formalise the appointment, which would be announced from 10 Downing Street that evening. The new Chairman, he confided, would be Charles Smith. He was hastily corrected by a Post Office official: 'Hill, Minister, Charles Hill.'

The appointment of a Chairman of the BBC, like other bodies operating under a Royal Charter, is made by the Queen in Council after a recommendation from the Prime Minister. I found out from the Privy Council a decade later that no extraordinary meeting, with five Privy Counsellors conveniently present in the Queen's box at Goodwood racecourse, had in fact taken place. Instead, Her Majesty had been put in the invidious position of having to approve the appointment of Lord Hill of Luton at a regular meeting of the Privy Council in Buckingham Palace two days after Downing Street had made the public announcement. The Lord President of the Council, R. H. S. Crossman, recorded in his diary, 'So Harold has coolly switched Hill to the BBC to discipline it and bring it to book, and above all to deal with Hugh Greene.'

Lusty hastened back to Broadcasting House to inform the Director-General. Sir Hugh Greene's immediate reaction was to resign. Cooler heads persuaded him that this would merely play into the Prime Minister's hand.

That evening Lord Hill hosted a dinner in honour of the retiring deputy chairman of the Independent Television Authority, Sir Sydney Caine. He kept silent about his new post until the end of the evening when he told the Authority members in his slow deliberative voice that he would be presiding at their meeting the next day for the last time. He had accepted another appointment which was inconsistent with remaining as chairman of the ITA. He then paused for a moment and added that he had accepted the chairmanship of the BBC Governors. The members of the Authority thought he was joking. Baroness Sharp said he used to show that quirky kind of humour when he was Minister of Housing and Local Government.

Lord Hill arrived at Broadcasting House to what he felt was a frosty reception. 'It's just another job,' he told Lusty. 'I can't make out what all the fuss is about.' Lusty said that was what all the fuss was about.

Five years later, when he retired at the end of 1972, having presided over the BBC's fiftieth anniversary celebrations, Lord Hill's critics had to admit that few of their original fears had materialised. The BBC had not been forced to take advertising. Indeed, the *Radio Times*, like the ITV companies before it, had had to forgo the lucrative advertising of cigarettes, under pressure from a Chairman whose career had started in medicine. Charles Hill was the son of a worker in a piano firm who had died when he was a baby. He won his way to Cambridge with scholarships and became the secretary of the British Medical

Association. He first achieved fame during the Second World War with his homespun broadcasts as the Radio Doctor.

Moreover, the Chairman had been a doughty fighter for the BBC's independence, resisting pressure to alter programmes from Labour over *Yesterday's Men* and from the Conservatives over *A Question of Ulster*. Those who were expecting a former Cabinet Minister to kowtow to erstwhile political colleagues over controversial programmes were pleasantly surprised.

Lord Hill's lively account of his work at the ITA and the BBC, *Behind the Screen*, published within a couple of years of leaving Broadcasting House, was criticised by several reviewers for revealing confidences, a practice Hill himself regarded as reprehensible in the case of junior staff making comparable leaks to the press. One example is his description of the impression made on himself and the other Governors by each candidate interviewed for the Director-Generalship. He even recorded the doubts of some Governors about the man they appointed, Charles Curran, and described his pension arrangements. Another breach of confidence was quoting from the minutes of the Board of Management.

Lord Hill had great energy and no lack of courage. Behind the owl-like face and portly body there was plenty of common sense and an earthy charm. He arrived with more broadcasting experience than any of his predecessors. He liked to regard himself as the first 'strong' BBC Chairman (see Wheldon, p. 189)

At the ITA he had also played a strong executive role. 'In future I am the Minister and Sir Robert Fraser (the Director-General) is the Permanent Under-Secretary,' he said on taking office in 1963, still in the language of Westminster. By that time he had been given a life peerage.

He forced reluctant programme companies to provide more airtime for ITN and established *News at Ten*. When the commercial franchises were reviewed in the spring of 1967 Hill did not hesitate to dump Television Wales and West, run from London by Lord Derby who had been one of the leading progenitors of commercial television, and to award the contract to Lord Harlech's rival group, more deeply rooted in Wales.

Lord Hill threatened similar treatment to Lord Thomson of Fleet, who had embarrassed ITV by referring to his Scottish Television franchise as 'a licence to print money'. Thomson countered with the threat that, if he lost STV, Hill would be responsible for the closing down of *The Times*. A compromise was reached after STV made sweeping changes. Other commercial television franchises were also altered.

Charles Hill had been Postmaster-General when ITV was founded. His political career had begun in 1950 with his election as the Liberal and Conservative member for Luton after giving an effective campaign broadcast during the General Election. With his deep distinctive voice and unconventional humour he had been a popular wartime broadcaster as the Radio Doctor ('Don't neglect the prunes – the little black-coated workers'). After only a year in the House of Commons Churchill appointed him Parliamentary Secretary to the Ministry of Food. Altogether Hill had spent ten years as a Minister and five in the Cabinet before being summarily dismissed by Macmillan, with six others, on 'the night of long knives', Friday 13 July 1962. Jeremy Thorpe, then the Liberal leader, commented, 'Greater love hath no man than this, that he lay down his friends for his life.'

At the time of Suez Charles Hill, by then Postmaster-General, had been the one minister who stuck up strongly for the rights of the BBC when it had earned Eden's displeasure. William Clark, the Downing Street public relations adviser, told me that Dr Hill had declared at the time that liver failure must be what was wrong with Eden's health, and it was affecting his judgement.

In the new Macmillan administration Charles Hill became Chancellor of the Duchy of Lancaster, with overall responsibility for government information. He mended the fences between Westminster and the BBC, and he was an effective general troubleshooter.

On the penultimate day of the 1958 Conservative Party Conference at Blackpool I invited Selwyn Lloyd, the Foreign Secretary, to be interviewed by Kenneth Harris in the BBC's television conference report, taking the precaution to confirm in writing the general areas the interview would cover, but stating clearly that there would be no possibility of submitting a list of the exact questions beforehand, as Lloyd had once demanded when he appeared on *Panorama*.

That evening there was a tense scene in the studio. Despite my letter, Selwyn Lloyd was insisting that it was highly irresponsible of Kenneth Harris not to tell him all his questions in advance, and threatening to walk out unless he did. Harris protested that in two weeks of interviewing frontbenchers at the Labour and Tory party conferences this was the first time anyone had asked to be slipped the questions beforehand. Both were getting hot under the collar. Eventually Selwyn Lloyd was persuaded to proceed and an interview took place which could not possibly have damaged Britain's international relations. But he left the studio in high dudgeon; clearly a row was brewing.

Later Kenneth Harris and I encountered the Chancellor of the Duchy of Lancaster in the conference hotel bar, and decided to seize the initiative by making a formal complaint about the behaviour of the Foreign Secretary. Charles Hill listened carefully to what had happened, puffing on his pipe, and bought a round of drinks, but he said little. The next day on Blackpool station he sidled up to me and said, 'I saw Selwyn Lloyd this morning, and I said "Selwyn, I hear you were a naughty boy in the BBC studio last night." And he blushed purple, and I reckon that's the end of the matter.' It was.

I end these sketches with Lord Hill because his appointment was a watershed which altered the course of the BBC, perhaps irretrievably. He upset the delicate balance between the Director-General and the Chairman, which materially affects the well-being of the Corporation, tipping it heavily in favour of the Chairman. Edward Heath told a group of American correspondents in 1973 that the main reason for appointing Sir Michael Swann as Hill's successor was to re-establish the position of the Director-General. Swann was one of the best Chairmen the BBC has ever had. But those who followed him, notably George Howard and Marmaduke Hussey, have reverted to the precedent established by Lord Hill of intervening in the day-to-day management of the BBC in a manner that would have been unthinkable in the days of Reith, Haley or Jacob.

Endpiece
There must be a better way

On 1 January 1927 the BBC became a public corporation operating under Royal Charter, a type of organisation then new in Britain. The original shareholders of the British Broadcasting Company Limited had been repaid, rather surprisingly at par. Without any expenditure of taxpayers' money the British nation acquired a well-established radio service, with all its capital equipment of transmitters, studios and broadcasting gear. It was worth a third of a million pounds and had all been financed out of revenue.

A fortnight earlier, at a dinner held to mark the change-over from private company to public corporation, Reith summarised the achievements of the original BBC. 'We have proved, as expected,' he declared, 'that the supply of good things creates the demand for more. We have tried to found a tradition of public service, and to dedicate the service of broadcasting to the service of humanity in its fullest sense. We believe that a new national asset has been created; not that kind of asset which brings credit entries to the books of the Exchequer.'

Those last words have developed a hollow ring in recent years. The BBC/ITV television duopoly used to be praised as a national asset, widely admired and envied by the rest of the world. It had managed to avoid both the jungle of unrestricted commercial rivalry and the dead hand of government control. BBC1 and ITV kept each other on their toes by competing on programme quality. They did not have to compete for income from the same source. Neither did ITV and Channel 4. Moreover, complementary television programming was provided by Channel 4 in the commercial sector and by BBC2 in the public-service sector. The British government, in its wisdom, decided to change all that.

Ever since television became the dominant medium of communication in the United Kingdom politicians have nourished a love–hate relationship with it. Supporters of the party in power tend to assume that its television image, rather than its policies and record, holds the key to victory at the next general election. Professional image-makers are increasingly employed. Their efforts are often undermined by programmes that draw attention to matters which governments prefer to keep under wraps. This is true of most television services in the Free World.

After the redistribution of the franchises of the ITV programme companies at the end of December 1980, Lord Thomson of Monifieth, the incoming chairman of the Independent Broadcasting Authority, commented sadly, 'There must be a better way.' In the event an even worse way was devised by the Thatcher administration in 1991. For the programme companies bidding for franchises it took the form of Russian roulette. The aim was to bring the maximum 'credit entries to the books of the Exchequer', to use Reith's words, while providing no discernible benefit to television viewers. Even Margaret Thatcher herself telephoned TVAM to apologise when it was put out of business as a consequence of this ill-considered policy.

The BBC has also suffered at the hands of recent governments. During the last two decades its independence has been threatened by official proposals from both Labour and the Conservatives. Harold Wilson had an obsessive feeling that the BBC was biased against him. He was particularly furious at being asked by David Dimbleby in the programme *Yesterday's Men* about the remuneration he had received from *The Sunday Times* for the sale of his memoirs. *Yesterday's Men*, a 1971 television documentary on the impact on the Labour Party of losing office, caused much offence to the Labour front bench. It had not been lived down seven years later when a Labour government White Paper, published after the Annan Report, proposed the creation of three 'service management boards' to supervise the programme strategy and management of Radio, Television and the External Services. Half the members of these service management boards were to be nominees of the government. Fortunately this quango scheme was derided on all sides and quietly withdrawn.

During the years of the Thatcher administration investigative television programmes, plus a number of own goals, made the BBC as unpopular with the Conservatives as it had been with Labour. Official resentment took various forms. One was pressure to make programmes toe the government line, as when Norman Tebbit openly impugned the integrity of Kate Adie's reporting from Libya.

More serious was the action, taken in two stages, to reduce the BBC's licence income to well below the level of inflation for television production. This deliberate underfunding of the licence fee was a serious body blow to public service television, driving the BBC into more and more quasi-commercial activities that give the appearance of privatisation by the back door. In a country such as the United Kingdom an adequately funded licence fee, indexed against inflation, provides the best way to finance a public service broadcasting organisation as well as giving it the most reliable protection against commercial or governmental pressure.

Consider the alternatives: a mixed system of licence fee and advertising, as in New Zealand, has the effect of gradually making the public service broadcaster become more and more commercial. When additional income is required, as is inevitable in these days of rising international costs, the broadcaster is told to take more advertising, and to drop minority public service programmes which do not readily attract sponsors.

Where, for demographic reasons, a freely contributed licence fee is difficult to collect, as in Canada and Australia, the public broadcaster has to be supported by government grant, with all the dependence on government goodwill which that involves. In the United States the public broadcasting system has to rely on a mixture of grants from Federal or State governments, sponsorship by public-spirited oil companies and the constant broadcasting of fund-raising appeals to its essentially middle-class audiences. It is impossible to establish a licence fee system in a country which has never had one. By the same token it is foolhardy to jeopardise a method which has worked well for over seventy years. Once abandoned it could never be reinstated.

The level of the licence fee in the United Kingdom did not provide a serious problem for the BBC so long as television audiences were still increasing, and prices remained stable. The steady growth of the number of licences bought covered most of BBC Television's rising costs, caused by having to compete against a wealthier network for artists and programme rights. However, when inflation became rampant, and the natural growth of income ceased, because most households in the country were already buying a licence, the BBC was thrown onto the mercy of the government of the day, for it alone had the power to revise the level of the licence fee. Moreover, an adequate level of licence fee only remains viable while the BBC continues to broadcast programmes that command a substantial share of the viewing audience. That is why the BBC has to resist the pressure to become an elitist service and nothing else.

In the last two decades British governments – whether Labour, Lib-Lab or Conservative – have been reluctant to maintain the purchasing power of the television licence fee, somehow fearing that to put up the licence to the figure needed might be the last straw that would lose a close-fought general election. Recent polls and research by the London Business School show that this is a groundless fear.

In my view the problem could be easily solved if the BBC and the government would express the licence fee in terms which are easily comparable with other expenditure on home entertainment, not as an increasingly unacceptable yearly figure, nor as a daily figure, which is too clever by half. Families who rent a television set or a video-recorder, or who subscribe to cable television or a satellite film channel, pay by the month, not by the year or by the day, and so naturally they think of such costs in monthly terms.

As I write the current licence fee, expressed as a monthly figure, is £6.92, shortly to become £7.04. To get two television channels, five national radio networks and a host of local radio stations for £7 compares very favourably with having to pay £14 to rent a video-recorder or

£20 to receive a satellite channel. And if because of inflation that figure should have to be raised to £7.50 or even £8 it would still look very good value by comparison. But the idea that the television licence should rise to over £100 horrifies many politicians. Expressing the licence fee as a monthly cost and one much lower than other similar expenditures, would remove these psychological inhibitions. It would also safeguard the invaluable licence fee system.

The government's direction to the broadcasters, taken for essentially ideological reasons, to farm out a quarter of their programme output to independent producers failed, in my view, to provide a spate of splendid new programme ideas to enrich the schedules of BBC1 and BBC2. Of course it provided more work for independent producers. It also resulted in many of the ablest BBC producers leaving the staff to become independents. Whether it is good for the long-term welfare of the Corporation to lose so many of its creative staff, while gaining scores of extra accountants, middle managers and minders, remains to be seen. Programmes are created by ideas, not by managerial directives.

In any large organisation there is always a risk that money may be wasted. But, as David Attenborough and others have forcefully pointed out, the BBC's cost efficiency in using its own studio facilities and other infrastructure has compared favourably with all other major broadcasters. The attempt to offset the underfunding of the licence fee by a labyrinthine system of internal accounting known as Producer Choice is one of the reasons for the perceived drop in BBC staff morale. Some have defined and dismissed Producer Choice as a 'cock-up'.

The emphasis has been on cost efficiency rather than

on nurturing creative and imaginative achievement. There has been an arbitrary cut in ancillary public service activity, such as engineering research, the archives and the History of Broadcasting Unit. Many small transactions inside the BBC generate a ludicrous amount of paperwork.

The BBC's Charter is due for renewal in 1996. I hope that Parliament will pay particular attention to the role of the Board of Governors. Under its first Charter the BBC had five Governors. Under its second the number was raised to seven. The Beveridge Committee recommended adding National Governors for Scotland, Wales and Northern Ireland and the total was raised to nine, already a somewhat unwieldy size for an effective Board. In 1966 Harold Wilson had been threatened with the mass resignation of the Board of Governors, as well as the Director-General, if Tony Benn's plan for the BBC to accept advertising on the Light Programme was imposed. Determined to prevent a repetition of such a unanimous threat, Wilson two years later increased the number of Governors to twelve.

The Chairman of the BBC Governors is appointed by the Queen in Council and does not resign if there is a change of government. With this in mind, Sir Alec Douglas-Home as Prime Minister made a point of making sure that Lord Normanbrook's name was acceptable to the Leader of the Opposition before recommending to the Queen his appointment as BBC Chairman. But that precedent has recently been ignored, and both Harold Wilson's choice of Lord Hill and Margaret Thatcher's of Marmaduke Hussey were actually announced from 10 Downing Street before they had been submitted to Her Majesty. Discourtesy apart, it would be good if a better system of selecting Governors were incorporated into the next Charter, as well as a reduction of their numbers to a more efficient size.

It is commonly said that the most important task of the Governors is to appoint the Director-General. It was odd, to put it mildly, that Marmaduke Hussey and his colleagues should have announced the promotion of John Birt from the post of Deputy Director-General to Director-General twenty-one months before Sir Michael Checkland was due to retire. The post was not advertised. Others, who had a strong claim to be considered, were not made aware of the vacancy suddenly brought forward. Even more astonishing was that anyone should think it proper to delegate the authority of the BBC's Director-General to a private company, one which paid for John Birt's Armani suits and employed his wife as a director and as a secretary.

When an enterprising journalist brought this unsavoury situation to light John Birt sought to limit the damage by joining the staff. This incident was a serious initial handicap for one who was planning to make unpopular decisions, involving many staff redundancies. But it also cast serious doubts on the judgement of those who saw nothing wrong in sanctioning this tax avoidance arrangement when they brought him in as Deputy Director-General in 1987.

The British people have been well served by the BBC in the past, and deserve to be well served in the future. Parliament can assure that future for the period of the next Charter if it firmly establishes certain ground rules. I believe they should include the following concepts.

The BBC must remain a popular universal service, providing something for everyone, rather than being limited to the 'higher ground' of elitist broadcasting. Major national sports events such as Wimbledon, which have previously been available to the whole population, must not be restricted to a satellite channel.

The BBC should be financed by an adequate, index-linked licence fee expressed as a monthly figure. Sponsorship and advertising must be rejected, and its editorial freedom from political interference should be legally protected. It ought to be the broadcaster's decision, not the government's, who it is proper to interview, and who not.

The trustees of the national interest should be a smaller Board of Governors, chosen for staggered terms on a bipartisan basis, and headed by a wise Chairman who is not tempted to get involved in day-to-day management.

Above all, it must be recognised that the BBC in the future, as in the past, will depend on the quality of its personnel. Leadership and concern for subordinate staff, as provided by Huw Wheldon and Paul Fox, integrity of the calibre found in David Attenborough's natural history series, programme humanity combined with the humour of a Gerald Priestland or a Ludovic Kennedy, steadfast defence of the BBC's political independence such as Ian Jacob and Hugh Greene showed, the professional expertise and courage of a Richard Dimbleby or a Robin Day – these, rather than tidy accountancy, will be the BBC's principal needs as it enters the new century.

Acknowledgements

The decade that I spent in the History of Broadcasting Unit working with Asa Briggs on various volumes of the BBC's official history helped me to place my own experience in a wider context. I owe a great debt to his stimulating approach to the complexities of BBC history. I am also most grateful for much help received from the other members of the History Unit, John Cain and Pat Spencer. The recent Management decision to abolish that useful and inexpensive activity is a sad reflection of current BBC priorities with regard to its public service obligations.

I have been a regular reader of the *Independent* since its first number in 1986. I warmly welcome the generous space given to the obituary notices that appear in its pages, for they are often the first drafts of history. Moreover, the Obituaries Editor, James Fergusson, has revolutionised the presentation of these notices in the British broadsheet newspapers. Tributes in the *Independent* invariably bear a signature. There are photographs often of a spectacular size or presented in an unusual manner. The range of lives recorded has transcended the conventional picture of the great and the good. Also there is a supplementary summary of the basic biographical facts. These Fergusson innovations have since been copied, in greater or lesser degree, by the other newspapers.

In 1987 James Fergusson asked me to write an obituary of Sir

Hugh Greene. Since then I have had many requests from him to write about other British broadcasting characters. I am grateful to the *Independent* for the use of earlier versions of some of the sections in this book.

To supplement my personal knowledge of these broadcasters I have consulted the following books:

Asquith, Margot, *Off the Record*, Frederick Muller, 1943.

Attenborough, David, *The Zoo Quest Expeditions*, Lutterworth Press, 1980.

Barry, Michael, *From the Palace to the Grove*, Royal Television Society, 1992.

Black, Peter, *The Mirror in the Corner*, Hutchinson, 1972.

—— *The Biggest Aspidistra in the World*, BBC, 1972.

Boyle, Andrew, *Only the Wind Will Listen: Reith of the BBC*, Hutchinson, 1972.

Briggs, Asa, *History of Broadcasting in the United Kingdom*, Volumes I–IV, Oxford University Press 1961, 1965, 1970, 1979.

—— *Governing the BBC*, BBC, 1979.

—— *The BBC: The First Fifty Years*, Oxford University Press, 1985.

Briggs, Asa, & Spicer, Joanna, *The Franchise Affair*, Century, 1986.

Cain, John, *The BBC: 70 years of broadcasting*, BBC, 1992.

Clark, Kenneth, *Civilisation: a personal view*, BBC and John Murray, 1969.

Cooke, Alistair, *A Generation on Trial*, Knopf, 1950.

—— *One Man's America*, Knopf, 1952.

—— *Alistair Cooke's America*, BBC, 1973.

—— *Six Men*, Knopf, 1977.

Cox, Geoffrey, *See it Happen: The Making of ITN*, Bodley Head, 1983.

Dictionary of National Biography 1951–60; 1961–70; 1971–80, Oxford University Press.

Dimbleby, Jonathan, *Richard Dimbleby: a biography*, Hodder & Stoughton, 1975.

Dougall, Robert, *In & Out of the Box*, Collins and Harvill, 1973.

Day, Robin, *Television: A Personal Report*, Hutchinson, 1961.

—— *Day by Day*, William Kimber, 1975.

—— *Grand Inquisitor*, Weidenfeld & Nicolson, 1989.

—— *... But with Respect*, Weidenfeld & Nicolson, 1993.

Eckersley, Peter, *The Power behind the Microphone*, Jonathan Cape, 1941.

Ferris, Paul, *Sir Huge: The Life of Huw Wheldon*, Michael Joseph, 1990.

Goldie, Grace Wyndham, *Facing the Nation*, Bodley Head, 1977.

Grisewood, Harman, *One thing at a time*, Hutchinson, 1968.

Greene, Sir Hugh, *The Third Floor Front*, Bodley Head, 1969.

Harding, Gilbert, *Along My Line*, Putnam, 1953.

Hibberd, Stuart, *'This – is London ...'*, Macdonald & Evans, 1950.

Hill, Lord, *Behind the Screen*, Sidgwick & Jackson, 1974.

Hudson, Robert, *Inside Outside Broadcasts*, R & W Publications (Newmarket), 1993.

Kennedy, Ludovic, *10 Rillington Place*, Gollancz, 1961.

—— *The Airman & the Carpenter*, Collins, 1985.

—— *On My Way to the Club*, Collins, 1989.

Lusty, Sir Robert, *Bound to be Read*, Cape, 1975.

Mansell, Gerard, *Let Truth be Told*, Weidenfeld & Nicolson, 1982.

Maschwitz, Eric, *No Chip on My Shoulder*, Herbert Jenkins, 1957.

McIntyre, Ian, *The Expense of Glory: A life of John Reith*, Harper Collins, 1993.

Miall, Leonard (ed), *Richard Dimbleby, Broadcaster*, BBC, 1966.

Michelmore, Cliff & Metcalfe, Jean, *Two-Way Story*, Elm Tree Books, 1986.

Milne, Alasdair, *DG: The Memoirs of a British Broadcaster*, Hodder & Stoughton, 1988.

Milner, Roger, *Reith: The BBC Years*, Mainstream Publishing, 1983.

Norden, Denis, Harper, Sybil & Gilbert, Norma, *Coming to you Live!* Methuen, 1965.

Potter, Jeremy, *Independent Television in Britain*, Volumes 3 & 4, Macmillan, 1989 & 1990.

Priestland, Gerald, *Something Understood*, Arrow Books, 1986.

Richardson, General Sir Charles, *From Churchill's Secret Circle to the BBC*, Brassey's (UK), 1991.

Russell, Audrey, *A Certain Voice*, Ross Anderson Publications, 1984.

Sendall, Bernard, *Independent Television in Britain*, Volumes 1 & 2, Macmillan, 1982 & 1983.

Simon of Wythenshawe, Lord, *The BBC from Within*, Gollancz, 1953.

Sinden, Donald, *Laughter in the Second Act*, Hodder & Stoughton, 1985.

Snagge, John & Barsley, Michael, *Those Vintage Years of Radio*, Pitman, 1972.

Stuart, Charles (ed.), *The Reith Diaries*, Collins, 1975.

Trethowan, Ian, *Split Screen*, Hamish Hamilton, 1984.

Tracey, Michael, *A Variety of Lives: A Biography of Sir Hugh Greene*, Bodley Head, 1983.

Wheldon, Huw (ed.), *Monitor*, Macdonald, 1962.

In addition I have quoted from a letter from Guy Hadley in the *Daily Telegraph* of 17 January 1977, from articles by Lionel Gamlin in the *Spectator* of 17 February 1956, Sir Robert Lusty in the *New Statesman* of 6 September 1974 and Hugh Burnett in the *Listener* of 20 October 1988.

The illustrations all come from the BBC's Photographic Library. I am most grateful to Margaret Kirby, the Library's Manager, and to Bobbie Mitchell for help in their selection.

Sir Robin Day suggested the idea for this book, during a lunch in generous settlement of a rash bet he made with me. I record my gratitude to him and also to Ion Trewin, a splendid editor as well as publisher. His colleague at Weidenfeld and Nicolson, Rosemary Legge, has provided much detailed help, for which I am most grateful.

Index

279